T0358724

Children from the Other America

TRANSGRESSIONS: CULTURAL STUDIES AND EDUCATION

Cultural studies provides an analytical toolbox for both making sense of educational practice and extending the insights of educational professionals into their labors. In this context *Transgressions: Cultural Studies and Education* provides a collection of books in the domain that specify this assertion. Crafted for an audience of teachers, teacher educators, scholars and students of cultural studies and others interested in cultural studies and pedagogy, the series documents both the possibilities of and the controversies surrounding the intersection of cultural studies and education. The editors and the authors of this series do not assume that the interaction of cultural studies and education devalues other types of knowledge and analytical forms. Rather the intersection of these knowledge disciplines offers a rejuvenating, optimistic, and positive perspective on education and educational institutions. Some might describe its contribution as democratic, emancipatory, and transformative. The editors and authors maintain that cultural studies helps free educators from sterile, monolithic analyses that have for too long undermined efforts to think of educational practices by providing other words, new languages, and fresh metaphors. Operating in an interdisciplinary cosmos, *Transgressions: Cultural Studies and Education* is dedicated to exploring the ways cultural studies enhances the study and practice of education. With this in mind the series focuses in a non-exclusive way on popular culture as well as other dimensions of cultural studies including social theory, social justice and positionality, cultural dimensions of technological innovation, new media and media literacy, new forms of oppression emerging in an electronic hyperreality, and postcolonial global concerns. With these concerns in mind cultural studies scholars often argue that the realm of popular culture is the most powerful educational force in contemporary culture. Indeed, in the twenty-first century this pedagogical dynamic is sweeping through the entire world. Educators, they believe, must understand these emerging realities in order to gain an important voice in the pedagogical conversation.

Without an understanding of cultural pedagogy's (education that takes place outside of formal schooling) role in the shaping of individual identity – youth identity in particular – the role educators play in the lives of their students will continue to fade. Why do so many of our students feel that life is incomprehensible and devoid of meaning? What does it mean, teachers wonder, when young people are unable to describe their moods, their affective affiliation to the society around them. Meanings provided young people by mainstream institutions often do little to help them deal with their affective complexity, their difficulty negotiating the rift between meaning and affect. School knowledge and educational expectations seem as anachronistic as a ditto machine, not that learning ways of rational thought and making sense of the world are unimportant.

But school knowledge and educational expectations often have little to offer students about making sense of the way they feel, the way their affective lives are shaped. In no way do we argue that analysis of the production of youth in an electronic mediated world demands some "touchy-feely" educational superficiality. What is needed in this context is a rigorous analysis of the interrelationship between pedagogy, popular culture, meaning making, and youth subjectivity. In an era marked by youth depression, violence, and suicide such insights become extremely important, even life saving. Pessimism about the future is the common sense of many contemporary youth with its concomitant feeling that no one can make a difference.

If affective production can be shaped to reflect these perspectives, then it can be reshaped to lay the groundwork for optimism, passionate commitment, and transformative educational and political activity. In these ways cultural studies adds a dimension to the work of education unfilled by any other sub-discipline. This is what *Transgressions: Cultural Studies and Education* seeks to produce – literature on these issues that makes a difference. It seeks to publish studies that help those who work with young people, those individuals involved in the disciplines that study children and youth, and young people themselves improve their lives in these bizarre times.

Children from the Other America

A Crisis of Possibility

Edited by

Michele López-Stafford Levy
New Mexico State University, USA

SENSE PUBLISHERS
ROTTERDAM/BOSTON/TAIPEI

A C.I.P. record for this book is available from the Library of Congress.

ISBN: 978-94-6300-445-9 (paperback)
ISBN: 978-94-6300-446-6 (hardback)
ISBN: 978-94-6300-447-3 (e-book)

Published by: Sense Publishers,
P.O. Box 21858,
3001 AW Rotterdam,
The Netherlands
https://www.sensepublishers.com/

Chapter 2 was originally published as
"The Trouble with English", Chapter Five in *From a Place in El Paso*, Gloria López-Stafford, 1996, University of New Mexico Press. Reprinted here with permission.

Chapter 8 was originally published as
Duncan-Andrade, J. (2009). Note to educators: Hope required when growing roses. *Harvard Educational Review*, Vol. 79, pp. 181–194. All rights reserved. Boston: Harvard University. Reprinted here with permission.

Cover photograph by Michele López-Stafford Levy © 2015

Printed on acid-free paper

TABLE OF CONTENTS

ACKNOWLEDGEMENTS

Our vision for this book is a collection of art and artifacts—filled with invaluable contributions from rock star scholars like Chomsky, López-Stafford and Duncan-Andrade. Art is sustenance for the soul especially when we are so thirsty for goodness and nonviolence in the world. We hope to share stories, narratives, poems, scholarship and photographs as a mindful assembly to create art.

This book became a vision first, then a reality supported by our Executive Editor Shirley Steinberg and Michel Lokhorst at Sense Publishers.

Rosie Castro-Feinberg is an icon in south Florida and insisted Esq. Peter Roos from Multicultural Education and Training Advocacy (META) tell the story in celebration of twenty-five years of the Florida Consent Decree (1990). Things began to snowball and artists began to coalesce. Celia Roberts (www.celiaroberts.com) our photographer from Colorado joined me and Carolyn O'Gorman-Fazzolari and Benito Fazzolari to document the memorial march for the slain Guatemalan young man named Marcelino in Jupiter, Florida. Suddenly we had a story to share, a memorial to attend, a call for calm and non-violence at the march in May of 2015, a month after this horrific hate crime. Very polished men in sunglasses joined us, chewing gum and even though they were Latino, seemed to be strangers in town because hate crimes are being hushed in the farms and fields of south Florida—folks are undocumented and so we'd like to empower them with a dedication to the people who put food on our tables and clean up after us at restaurants and mow our lawns. People who live in the shadows except when you need labor.

Fr. Frank O'Loughlin is a veritable living saint among us and has made south Florida his home since 1965. I like to call Padre "the real deal" because you meet so few of them in your life and yet you know you are with pure goodness when you meet a saint. Radical priests are present in slums, ghettos, barrios and rural areas and Padre Frank was with Cesar Chavez on behalf of farmworkers back in the day. When I met Frank I was inspired to write the book, pull together the team and dedicate it to hard working people who live in the shadows of ANY industrialized nation.

The cover photograph was taken in Immokalee, Florida which is famous for fair wage for tomato corporate farms and their challenges in times past. Immokalee is a symbol of Taco Bell finally paying tomato workers a decent wage. The symbolism of the bicycles was too hard to ignore as we passed by them because undocumented workers cannot have driver's licenses and so they go to work on buses and leave their bikes chained together all day at the bus stop. To add insult to injury, farmworkers must ride a bicycle home (farm roads) after a hard day of working in the fields where buses transport them. The chained bicycles are symbolic for farmworker's chained lives yet strength in numbers too.

Thank you one and all for an incredible year of crisis and contemplation. There are many communities around the world with large influxes of refugees and we'd like to share how communities in the U.S. mobilized.

Visit us on: https://www.facebook.com/childrenfromtheotherAmerica/

MICHELE LÓPEZ-STAFFORD LEVY

1. INTRODUCTION

Policy makers, the public and the media were seemingly caught off guard in spring 2014 when a surge of child migrants from Central America reached the U.S. Mexico border in unprecedented numbers. (Migrant Policy Institute, 2014)

Imagine if you will a mist settling on the lush jungle floor and wise, old Mother Earth rumbles and tumbles and the land cracks and rolls and she painfully groans as her children once again wage war amongst themselves. An ensuing exodus from Central America has happened again.

The year was 2014, the month was June and suddenly it seemed like almost every school in the U.S. witnessed an influx of new students at the end of the school year from Central America. Bill O'Reilly callously proclaimed in July of 2014, We're not a "dumping ground!" upon the news of child refugees at our doorstep. He seethed, "We can't take care of the world's poor" (July, 2014) mugging and miming quotation marks for the camera every time he said "refugees". As orators know, the power of repetition is memorable for audiences. In that speech (YouTube), three times, O'Reilly says "refugees" miming his quotation fingers.

The reality is, the unaccompanied children are refugees. They come from desperate circumstances and here, many of them become the lowest rung on the ladder of success in the land of milk and honey. Donald Trump says, "I love Mexicans. They do a great job on my lawn" with his Manhattan accent. Jon Stewart calls Trump "a gift" to the Democratic Party. Latino/Hispanos just call him asshole (*culero*).

There is no denial every industrialized nation needs immigrant labor. Undocumented workers do the nasty, grueling and menial jobs no Northern American wants to do and furthermore, in Florida, city officials cordon off their Guatemalan community in both Jupiter and Lake Worth as well as Immokalee to the west on the Florida Everglades. This is where the Seminole tribe was ultimately banished and ironically sits on a gold mine—the Florida Everglades, the port of Miami and Fort Lauderdale for cruise lines, hotels and tourism. The wheels of justice are slow but they grind ever so finely. All those twenty dollar bills with Andrew Jackson on them are spinning in the fat wallets of U.S. citizens spending big bucks in Seminole Casinos. Cha ching! Poetic justice!

In this creative collection are a variety of narratives, poems, short stories and scholarly articles with attempts to honor in artistic ways the unaccompanied

M. López-Stafford Levy (Ed.), Children from the Other America, 1–11.

children, the work of farm labor and the Guatemala Mayan communities of south Florida. Our sole focus is on the plight of children and families unable to fully engage in a community—unable to get a driver's license. To even further isolate the Guatemalan Maya Indian in communities leaving them stripped and powerless with no ability to drive—no recognition of international driver's licenses (cover photo), no clear path to citizenship nor recognition of refugee status because the U.S. does not recognize the drug wars in the Northern Triangle worthy of refugee status. Just like Bill O'Reilly.

Thirty years ago there was a drug war of epic proportions in Central America. Cultural anthropologist J. P. Linstroth (2004) a scholar and fellow activist documented the depositions of Guatemalans fleeing in droves to the U.S. in the 1980's and described the scorched and abandoned Mayan villages in the jungles of Guatemala as being annihilated. Linstroth reports, "Mayan babies were being bandied about like soccer balls" by *ladino* soldiers (p. 27). Another narrative describes babies "melting on stones like oil" (p. 28).

We offer no apologies about these graphic images but rather propose them to serve as memory palaces—to remember and pay homage to all of our immigrant and native ancestors alike. We come to the U.S. for various reasons—some under circumstances more desperate than others.

Fast forward thirty years to the summer of 2014, as "*La Bestia*" (the train known as "the beast") rolls into Mexico delivering desperate people to even more desperate circumstances at our southwestern most border. *La bestia* was but one of many ways our nation's thousands of refugees arrived in the summer of 2014.

Needless to say, because of the surge in unaccompanied children, the backlog of immigration court dockets in places like Texas, Arizona and California were unable to process refugees in a timely manner and operated at full throttle and maximum capacity as immigrants and newcomers alike escaped the unthinkable violence back home in Central America.

One can't help but ask, who are these women and children and who did they leave behind? Who do they know when they reach their family in the U.S.? What about the completely unaccompanied minor? What then? Can we grow roses in the concrete (Duncan-Andrade, 2009)?

This eclectic collection of artifacts knits together a snapshot in time when immigrants from Central America arrived at our borders weaving a tapestry of narratives—both scholarly and aesthetically (Greene, 1980). We weave threads from Web 2.0 narratives/blogs/posts among scholarly research interspersed with poetry/literature from the academic fields of Chicana/Chicano Studies (López-Stafford) liberatory education (Duncan-Andrade) and critical pedagogy (O'Gorman-Fazzolari). In honor of the symbolism of the weaver's loom for native indigenous/aboriginal peoples, we attempt to weave a story in honor of your incredible personal narratives of survival and disaster, about human trafficking of both boys and girls and inconceivable accounts of resiliency (Final Chapter).

In our time capsule filled with snapshots of immigrant accounts (Stafford-Levy, 2004) our work shares photos, recordings, interviews, transcripts and original research attempting to re-tell stories about activism by sharing narratives through our lens as scholars, community members, grassroots activism, teachers of this population we serve in south Florida and even the powerful work of the clergy and liberatory theologians like Fr. Frank O'Loughlin of south Florida—a radical priest working with farmworkers for more than forty years now.

Like Foucault, Avi Chomsky looks at the "master narrative" of post-colonial Mesoamerican history and creatively slices up the U.S. immigration pie into four acts as a dramatic essay in our extremely diverse collection. This editor watched an online recording of Avi at a conference workshop in Austin, Texas. There were Mexican-Americans speaking on stage who were more comfortable using highly academic Spanish and sharing concepts about activism. Finally the interpreter waved their hand, stepped off the stage and let Dr. Chomsky take over—no middleman needed. The daughter of Noam Chomsky is perfectly bilingual in Spanish and did the interpreting herself while serving as plenary speaker—double duty a lot like our bilingual students. Truly remarkable. We are delighted to share her wonderful, original contribution to this anthology.

It is an interesting anecdote the way this book emerged which came from pleas posted on a professional listserv (FLSSTESOL @Yahoo Groups) for help from educators like Dr. Mercedes Pichard who teaches the unaccompanied refugees in a high school near Immokalee however in Lee County and a professor in a local teacher preparation as well. The editor of this anthology serves on the Executive Board of Directors of SSTESOL (Florida's Sunshine State Teaching English to Speakers of Other Languages) with Dr. Pichard who posted in the spring of 2014:

This Quiche student will not stop crying and he's sixteen years old. The entire school has been traumatized and his classmates are upset as well and no one knows exactly what to do. (Blog Artifact)

It became apparent, some of these children were suffering from post-traumatic stress disorder (PTSD) and suddenly an overwhelming need for Quiche speaking mental health practitioners befell the communities of Dade, Broward, Palm Beach County and Lee to name but a few.

Some of our conversations with the students in these overwhelmed schools spoke of calloused, mean and insensitive teachers, especially when it came to test scores for immigrants. As life would have it, the trauma manifest in the classrooms, out in the school yards and into the community culminating in a horrific hate crime in Palm Beach County in April of 2015. We deliberately have avoided the deficit model for this collection. We choose to honor our dead and the community they live in and the schools and churches who have come together in a time of crisis. It does take a village—and a fairly tenacious one, at that.

Gloria López-Stafford shares the story of Yoya in *A Place in El Paso* where you'll see the recurrent symbol of the street lamp in our anthology shedding light on the immigrant narrative.

Yoya and her band of *barrio* boys play under the street lamp in *la Tartana*—an old jalopy belonging to a Mexican-American soldier who never returned home to his beloved barrio from WWII. The Second Ward children played under the glow of a lamp in the *Segundo barrio's* cool nights after a hot summer day in El Paso/Juarez. Her chapter *The Trouble with English* is part of our collection emblematic of the voice of the immigrant child learning English and trying to find their place in the world and their own identity. The character Yoya was not really interested in learning the new language until she was motivated. There are many universal themes immigrant children share concerning bilingualism. For example, Yoya shares the phenomenon of losing her English over the summer and reminds us about the importance of identity and the immigrant experience. In other parts of her book, López-Stafford writes about the money boys who craned their necks below the bridge catching coins in large newspaper cones from pedestrians above. Rich literacy skills like these might not be recognized by white teachers in south Florida. Luis Moll (2015) calls them funds of knowledge urging educators to tap and mold like clay. This editor was a high school English teacher and says, "You just have to look for that special gift within each child-some a little harder than others".

Yet, *A Place in El Paso* demonstrates how schools can wound too (Olson, 2009). The Anglo teacher catches the girls speaking Spanish IN THE COAT CLOSET and punishes Yoya and Raquel from recess. This rich narrative from the perspective of an immigrant child deserves a special thank you for your contribution to our anthology and for sharing your story with the world.

Central American refugees endure an extremely perilous journey to the U.S. The Migration Policy Institute (2015) states between 2011 and 2014 the number of Central American children and "family units" (official terminology) surged and for parents traveling north but if you talk to any of the locals in this particular farming community of Immokalee, Florida where we visited, the community members all had incredible stories of determination and resiliency. While seated at a local lunch counter eating tacos in this very small farm town, one genteel lady in a maroon apron shared her story with us and the irony was not lost on me. Lunch counters are quite symbolic for my "g-g-generation".

Weeks before the hate crime in Charleston, South Carolina at Emanuel A.M.E Church, Reverend Clementa Pinkney's church, a hate crime took place in Jupiter, Florida. Local young men in the community conceived the racial slur "'Guat' hunting" referring to Guatemala Mayan living there. This is how "Marcelino" was referred to (see Hines poem) in a vicious, seemingly premeditated murder with a rock to the skull and even worse, the murder is being swept under the rug by local, conservative media. They even titled the article wrong in the local newspaper to further bury the story. City officials told Father Frank founder of the Guatemala Mayan Center in Lake Worth, Florida they didn't want another Ferguson on their hands.

A month after the murder of Marcelino, the locals (indigenous, Hispanic and Anglo American) memorialized him in a city-sponsored march by the mayor and local law enforcement agencies trying desperately to gain the trust of these undocumented immigrants.

While this book was being written and in a show of solidarity, three of this anthology's authors slowly and solemnly marched among television cameras and media in show of unity with those who live in the shadows. At the end of the march, participants gathered in the community park. With television cameras present, we took the opportunity to address the importance of non-violence in response to the murder as many Mayans, Mexicans and Central Americans stood in the crowd. A hushed gathering listened as the clergy, professors and community members called for calm and nonviolence and resolved to meet again about street lamps—a great place to start in a long line of safety concerns and issues by mothers from Central America living in Palm Beach County, Florida.

Figure 1. Memorial march for slain Guatemalan teen and gathering in the park
(© 2015 Celila Roberts)

In trying to secure popular activism within this mourning community of Jupiter, a young mother and budding community activist by the name of Isabel wearing a straw *hipster* hat and glasses spoke on behalf of the deeply saddened mothers at

Marcelino's memorial. She shouted loudly for the Sherriff to answer some questions. He waved his hand at Isabel and said, "No questions, no questions." So Isabel turned to her community and asked, "What can we do? What do we need? What do we want"? We dedicate this book to those who live in the shadows on streets with no street lamps. We dedicate this work to Marcelino.

Another community member by the name of Marlena (as in Dietrich) told us her son had earned a full ride to the University of Michigan and her eyes welled up with tears as she recounted her story of a three-day harrowing trek by foot when she first entered the U.S. with her toddler at her side. Marlena said she came here for a better life so that her son could have a real chance at life and a decent education. Her burgundy apron was clean and tidy and Marlena told us she cleaned the refugee center across the street and that she'd be here the next time we returned to visit the center called the Coalition of Immokalee Workers.

Immokalee, if you know your migrant rights history, is iconic for the rights of tomato workers. Back in the day, Cesar Chavez was unable to organize under United Farmworkers thanks to the gargantuan lobbying power of Florida's corporate farms and any hints of unionized labor were quickly snuffed by the giant companies and, out of necessity, the Immokalee Coalition of Workers was born. These tenacious laborers brought national and international attention to the need for decent and fair wages for the people who help bring food to our tables. Presently, the Coalition is boycotting grocery chains like Publix who ignore Fair Food efforts and post on their web site (www.ciw-online.org/) Fair Food Program participants like Trader Joe's and WalMart.

It's quite challenging to write books in these times of incredible change from moment to moment and day to day and so in order to not become quickly dated, our idea is to share stories close to our hearts after the influx of immigrants from Central America in the summer of 2014 and try to give voice to the voiceless who provide the beautiful vegetables and produce in our markets and work as bus boys and wait staff in restaurants. Every industrial society needs the working poor to perform the back-breaking, grueling and menial jobs no one else will do. Immokalee Florida has a long history of civil disobedience (see YouTube) and to unionize in the red state of Florida heretical thanks to strong lobby groups funded by corporate farms and so the Immokalee farmworkers created a coalition years ago and urged Americans to boycott the likes of Publix (Fair Food), Taco Bell (Yum Brands) and Minute Maid in the 1970's, '80's for a decent wage. Back in the day, tomatoes fetched thirty-five cents a bucket. To make $50.00, someone had to pick 2 tons of tomatoes.

Cesar Chavez' United Farmworkers was not allowed in the state of Florida. Chavez tried with our colleague, fellow activist and friend Fr. Frank O'Loughlin in Palm Beach County Florida and slept on his sofa during the really hard years. Nothing doing! Florida was not for Cesar Chavez. As Freire (1970) so aptly reminds us,

Men and women [sic] simultaneously create history and become historical beings. Because—in contrast to animals—people can tri-dimensionalize time into the past, the present and the future, their history, in function of their own creations, develop as a constant process of transformation within which epochal units materialize ... On the contrary, epochal units interrelate in the dynamics of historical continuity. (p. 82)

The editor Michele Stafford Levy wrote a play while a drama major during undergraduate school at LSU in the 1980's when the first drug wars broke out in Guatemala. Inspired by the now controversial Nobel Peace Prize recipient Rigoberta Menchu and based on the saying from Menchú Tum (2004):

The bones of the dead tell no lies. In many cases, they speak on their own behalf, telling stories of pain, violence, and abuse. In Guatemala, every clandestine cemetery that is found, every bone that is recovered from Mother Earth speaks of the people who were annihilated, of the homes burned, of the indiscriminate massacres. In short, they speak of the crimes against humanity, of the genocide committed by the army against the indigenous population. (Menchú Tum, 2004: 7)

The first scene of Michele's drama takes place in a Mayan jungle cemetery with an eerie fog hovering on a dimly lit stage—headstones under low spots. Suddenly agonizing howls from the ghosts of slain indigenous awaken to the drone of a weepy drum. Strangely, from the grave, like Shakespeare's Lear, the slain return from the dead to reveal the secrets of their atrocious deaths. And like our anthology's beginning, Mother Earth rolls over again and sobs for her babies.

Fast forward thirty years later, same stage different players. These poor characters (extended metaphor) journey through dangerous Mexican highways and end up in detention centers but by U.S. standards are NOT considered refugees. We write this book about the unaccompanied children who certainly are the most distressing of collateral damage from the Northern Triangle drug wars and, ironically, the country who consumes the drugs doesn't quite know what to do with the most vulnerable of the world's population—child refugees from Central America.

To add insult to injury, for-profit detention centers reveal the ugly, opportunistic face of U.S. corporate profiteering off the backs of women and children who are charged for food when the cafeteria fare purposively atrocious so they pay the canteen (prison owned), refugees pay the prison for phone calls and decent food and yet in Summer of 2015, the women and children organized an audacious protest in Dilley, Texas when federal officials visited. Meanwhile, the detention centers owned by the likes of the McCombs family of Texas embody American opportunism at its finest. Columbia University just severed its ties with its for-profit penal system association. Let's see if UT Austin can match Columbia University's pledge. McCombs school of Business might not appreciate a for-profit detention center relationship (Observer, 2015).

In our collection are two transcripts to capture narratives from the actors themselves. First we'll meet Jonathan Ryan (a "good attorney") of San Antonio's RAICES who leads this immigration law firm and held a press conference during a town hall style meeting as one of the largest surges of Central American refugees streamed across the borders. We share Jonathan's "live" speech to honor his great leadership abilities, eloquence with educating the public (mostly churches and charity groups) and mobilizing a community for the unaccompanied minors who "retain" legal counsel. Children must secure legal counsel once here in the U.S. and to hear children talk about their lawyers is stupefying.

Speaking of legal issues, if you've lived in south Florida for any amount of time and follow causes like LULAC and TESOL, you'll eventually hear about the legend of Rosie Castro-Feinberg. Rosie has the power to not only raise the waters but part them as well; to get people to help her pass laws for children who don't speak English. In 1990, language rights prevailed and the passage of the Florida Consent Decree was won. In honor of the twenty-fifth anniversary of the Florida Consent Decree supporting and honoring the rights of children who are learning English, we wanted to interview Rosie as the former Miami Dade school board member and she wouldn't hear of it. She directed us to Peter Roos one of our nation's top civil rights attorneys. *Tapestry*, a highly informative website by the University of South Florida for TESOL pre-service teachers lists Esq. Roos' lifetime achievements in the form of a timeline at http://tapestry.usf.edu/Roos/outline.html. We feel we've incorporated the Lau decision and the Civil Rights Movement in a creative and interesting way by offering the reader a primary source from the attorney responsible for a very important language rights law in Florida.

Quick facts where the Consent Decree came from:

- Title VI and VII Civil Rights Act of 1964
- Office of Civil Rights Memorandum (Standards for Title VI Compliance) of May 25, 1970
- Requirements based on the Supreme Court decision in Lau v. Nichols, 1974
- Equal Education Opportunities Act of 1974
- Requirements of the Vocational Education Guidelines, 1979
- Requirements based on the Fifth Circuit court decision in Castañeda v. Pickard, 1981
- Requirements based on the Supreme Court decision in Plyler v. Doe, 1982
- Americans with Disabilities Act (PL 94–142)
- Florida Education Equity Act, 1984
- Section 504 of the Rehabilitation Act of 1973

When school laws are in place, school teachers have been known to be activists. We had the opportunity to meet a teacher at the Florida State TESOL Conference who is originally from Guatemala. She is married to a fellow Guatemalan physician and lives in northern Florida. This advocate and school teacher for Central American students just quit her teaching job. Marta tells us her "contract was not renewed" because she defended the children and championed their causes. Marta was mortified when the cafeteria staff created problems for a young Guatemalan boy unfairly accused of "stealing chicken" in the lunch line (personal communication). We desperately need great teachers and the system seems to be failing them.

Recently, Donald Trump swiped a very, very broad brushstroke that Mexicans were rapists and drug lords. It hurts. Really. And so we dedicate this anthology with the passion Latinos have for art and drama, literature and poetry with "weavings" of photographs, scholarly writings from critical theorists and local activists. Incorporating Web 2.0 attempts to address the urgency of and critical nature of social networking hoping more and more of us use Web 2.0 artifacts as part of the larger narrative. We can make a change and therein lies possibility—a crisis of possibility and how to mobilize a community like Jonathan Ryan and the staff RAICES of San Antonio, Texas.

Henry Giroux (2011) believes we are in dire *crisis of ideas* and urges debate in our schools across this representative nation as tantamount to true democratic processes to model what years earlier Neil Postman (1969) suggested "teaching as a subversive activity" (p. 1) and Giroux (2004) further suggests "when hope is subversive" (p. 1). Let's get teachers involved in activism through debate about noble ideas like being good stewards of our beautiful planet and championing dignity and the rights of those who are marginalized. Either way, it is incumbent upon educators to keep Hegel's (2004) dialectic bulldozing forward with our very eager and energetic youth engaged in debates about social justice and democracy across our country and the very, very large discussion about what empowering education looks like (Freire, 1970) – especially for the Mesoamerican refugees in U.S schools, crowded adult education programs and those who are trapped in for-profit detention centers in the U.S. Europe now too has an influx of refugees (2016). We share a common challenge.

For Peter McLaren (1997), like Giroux, debates are critical to our conversation in a democracy calling them "engaged narratives" (p. 91). McLaren's development of revolutionary politics and the struggle for social justice is "not so much the politics of diversity as the global decentering and dismantling of whiteness" (p. 306). History will teach us how communities coalesce during huge influxes of immigrants no matter the country and whether the dominant culture is compassionate or repulsed and filled with xenophobia. Whether they embrace or whether they "other" folks, the crisis of possibility rests in the hands of the entirety of a democracy during surges of immigrants to new lands.

John Hines was so utterly and deeply moved by Marcelino's hate crime he penned this poem as a tribute to his life because all lives matter. Marcelino López' short life was cut short by haters and cut down by a crushing final blow to his Guatemala Mayan (Guat) skull.

HUNTING GUATS BY JOHN HINES

Walking Wakodahachee
Right there on the boardwalk
Below our feet
Purple gallinules – great yellow feet splayed –
We're gathering nesting shoots of green grass
You told me of that murder

Three kids about nineteen
Who taught them to hate?
They called themselves Guat hunters
One picked up a rock
One picked up an iron bar
And with heavy arms
They bludgeoned another kid
A Guatemalan immigrant
Who had fled the killings at home
Such ugliness amid such beauty!
I won't pass those gallinules again
Without anger
Without recalling
Hateful arms
The iron bar
That bloody rock

Children destroying children
What have we come to?

To Marcelino: Slain Mayan teenager,
Palm Beach County Florida Spring 2015

REFERENCES

American Immigration Council. (2015). *A guide to children arriving at the border: Laws, policies and responses.* Washington, DC: American Immigration Council.

Chavkin, N., & Feyl-Gonzalez, J. (2000). *Mexican immigrant youth and resiliency: Research and promising programs.* Washington, DC: National Center for Research on Teacher Learning (ERIC Document Reproduction Service No. ED447990).

Duncan-Andrade, J. (2009). Note to educators: Hope required when growing roses. *Harvard Educational Review, 79,* 181–194. Reprinted with Permission. All rights reserved. Boston, MA: Harvard University.

Freire, P. (1970). *A pedagogy of the oppressed.* New York, NY: Continuum.

Giroux, H. (2004). When hope is subversive. *Tikkum, 19*(6), 38–39.

González, N., Moll, L. C., & Amanti, C. (2005). *Funds of knowledge: Theorizing practices in households, communities, and classrooms.* Mahwah, NJ: Lawrence Erlbaum Associates.

Hegel, F. (2004). *The philosophy of history*. London: Dover.

Linstroth, J. P. (2009). Mayan cognition: A snapshot from the past. *History & Anthropology, 20*(2), 139–182.

López-Stafford, G. (1996). *A place in El Paso: A Mexican-American childhood*. Santa Fe, NM: University of New Mexico Press.

McLaren, P. (1997). *Revolutionary multiculturalism: Pedagogies of dissent for the new millennium*. Boulder, CO: Westview.

Menchú Tum, R. (2004), *Victims and witnesses*. In J. Moller (Ed.), *Our culture is our resistance: Repression, refuge, and healing in Guatemala*. New York, NY: Powerhouse Books.

Olson, K. (2009). *Wounded by schools*. New York, NY: Teachers College Press.

O'Reilly, B. (2014, June 6). *America is not a dumping ground – HEATED debate over illegal immigrant children*. Chicago, IL: Fox News.

Postman, N., & Weingartner, C. (1969). *Teaching as a subversive activity*. New York, NY: Delta.

Richardson, G. E., Neiger, B. L., Jenson, S., & Kumpfer, K. L. (1990). The resiliency model. *Health Education, 21*(6), 33–39.

Rodriguez, R. (2002). *Cantos al sexto sol: An anthology of Aztlanahuae writings*. San Antonio, TX: Wings Press.

Rosenblum, M. (2015). *Unaccompanied child migration to the United States: The tension between protection and prevention*. Washington, DC: Migration Policy Institute.

Stafford-Levy, M. (2002). *My introspective time capsule* (Networks: An online journal in teacher research, 12). Santa Cruz, CA: University of Santa Cruz. Retrieved October 31, 2004, from http://www.oise.utoronto.ca/%7Ectd/networks/journal/Vol%205%283%29.2002dec/Stafford-Levy.html

Trump, D. (2015). *Donald Trump FULL SPEECH: 2016 presidential campaign announcement June 16 at New York: Trump Tower*. Retrieved https://www.youtube.com/watch?v=0XXcPl4T55I

Wilder, F. (2015). *Feds planning massive family detention center in South Texas*. Retrieved from http://www.texasobserver.org/exclusive-feds-planning-massive-family-detention-center-south-texas/

GLORIA LÓPEZ-STAFFORD

2. THE TROUBLE WITH ENGLISH[1]

In the Segundo Barrio during the 1940's, people spoke Spanish. They spoke the Spanish they brought with them from their *ranchos*, villages and cities. They also brought the music of their accents. You could tell by the quality of their speech whether they were country or city people. Spanish in the 1940's in south El Paso was formal and polite. People apologized if they said a word like *estúpido*. I would often wonder why that required an apology. And I would be told that people from rural areas are not open with criticism and do not want to offend with what they consider vulgar language.

When people left the barrio, they began using English more. You still spoke Spanish at home because that was what your family used. Then when you spoke with someone who also spoke both languages, the language evolved to a mixture of English and Spanish that became an art form. Sometimes sentences might be in one language with certain words in the other. Other times whole paragraphs might be in one language and only a few sentences in the other. It was a living language, a musical score that conveyed the optimal sense, meaning and feeling from both languages that a single language might not achieve. The combination drew criticism from purists and people who did not speak both. They accused the bilingual person of being lazy or undisciplined. But I think it was a love of both languages that made it impossible to be faithful to just one. One the other hand, cussing or profanity were best in English. The words were just words to me. Cussing in Spanish was painful and created emotions that led to guilt. And, it was unacceptable to our parents and priests.

The first time I remember having problems with English was the year before Carmen came to live with us. At least once a week Palm and I would have a talk about why I wasn't learning English. I saw no reason to. I had to experience a need for it, and that is what happened.

"You have to learn English, Gloria," Palm would say.

"I don't want to. I don't have to. I don't need it," I would stubbornly refuse.

"I suppose you didn't need it at the border on Saturday when immigration held you after you were in Juárez with López and you couldn't answer their questions?" he said firmly. "I had to leave the store to go and get them to release you. All because you can't carry on a conversation in English".

I had created problems for Palm and myself, but I didn't want to learn English and that was that.

M. López-Stafford Levy (Ed.), Children from the Other America, 13–19.

On this particular morning, I waited for Palm to get tired of the topic and to move on to something else. But he didn't. He continued.

"The note the teacher sent home says that you will not speak English. She says that everyone speaks for you. And she says that you talk all the time, but in Spanish! It's been a month since school started and she says you will not cooperate. She says she is going to punish you. She wrote to inform me that she is at the end of her patience with you" Palm said.

"So that is what the *mugre*, dirty, note said. I thought she liked me," I said as I thought of how she and I grinned at each other every day. I didn't understand what she was saying and she didn't know what I was saying. She could have been speaking Chinese just like the Chinos near the Cuauhtemoc market in Juárez. I just didn't want to speak English.

"It sounds ugly. And I look stupid speaking it," I admitted when I saw Palm's face.

"It's because you don't use enough to get used to it," Palm tried to explain.

"My friends and I don't need it speak it. We have our own way of speaking." I continued the argument until I noticed that Palm was frustrated and quiet. I decided to play. I put my left hand on my hip and shook my right index finger menacingly.

"Wo do bo to do ri ra do fo, da mo meeester!" I said in gibberish. "Ha, no, meeeezter?" I raised my eyebrow and looked at Palm. "That's English!"

"*Payasa.* You are very stubborn. You need to learn English." Palm started up again. "My son is coming to visit and he speaks English."

The last remark caught my attention. I turned my eyes to the picture of Palm's son, which was displayed in a large oval frame. He resembled Palm. I wondered why he was only my half-brother. When I was younger, I thought it was because only the upper part of his body was in the picture. Palm corrected me. He told me his son had a different mother and was the only one of his children who stayed in touch with him. He loved Palm very much and would write to him every week. He was the youngest child and had been in college when my father went to Mexico. Palm's son's light eyes seemed to follow me around the room.

Palm was still talking about a visit from his son when I found my voice and said, "*¡Que suave!* When he comes, I'll tell him all about me and the neighborhood." Palm just nodded his head and gave me a strange look.

The next week, when I got home from school, I was frightened because I thought someone was in the apartment. But Palm called to me when I pressed my nose against the screen to look inside.

"*Entra, mi'ja.*" Palm's voice was happy. I pulled the screen door open and entered the living room. A man was with my father. He looked like my father but he wasn't old; he looked familiar. Then, suddenly, my eyes turned to the picture on the wall. I looked at the man and I looked at the picture. They were the same!

"*¡Hola! ¿Cómo estás?*" I yelled with happiness as I ran to hug the stranger. He returned the hug. I was overjoyed. Palm was telling the truth about his son coming to visit. Here he was...all of him!

14

Palm's son opened his mouth to say something and said something to Palm who was telling him something too. They were speaking Chinese!

"Apá, tell him that I speak Spanish," I told my father.

"Yoya, he knows." Palm spoke slowly because he knew how I would react. "He doesn't speak Spanish. He only speaks English. I told you many times."

I was speechless. What a dirty *trampa*, trick.

"Didn't you tell him I didn't speak English? Did you forget? I questioned my Palm as the other Palm looked on with the biggest and sweetest smile. How could he not speak Spanish? I started to cry, but the other Palm understood as my father told him in Chinese what the problem was. Palm's son laughed as he picked me up and kissed me and said something to my father. I looked to Palm for a translation.

"He said you're as precious as he knew you would be. He's sorry that he can't speak Spanish. He has never been able to learn," my father said.

I hugged his son and just watched them as they talked. Occasionally, Palm would tell me what they were saying if he thought it might interest me. I just kept looking into the visitor's beautiful face. My little chest was heavy with the weight of my broken heart. I had so wanted to be able to talk with him. I couldn't believe it. And I knew Palm had warned me.

When the sunset, the color of a West Texas sweet potato flesh, began to spread across the barrio, our visitor said he had to leave. We went outside. Palm's son picked me up and kissed me. Palm softly told me what his saying to me.

"He says he loved you, Yoya. He hopes that when you meet again, either you'll know English or he'll know Spanish."

I hugged and kissed my favorite visitor back. It would be many years before I would see him again and it would be long after my father's death. But on this evening, my father and I watched him as he walked to Virginia Street where he had parked his car. Palm and I sat on the cement step. As the car pulled off with my half-brother, I turned to Palm and said with determination and sadness,

"It's time I learned English, Papí."

"*Sí corazón*, yes." He understood.

English continued to be a problem for me for the next few years. In September of 1945, after Carmen came to live with us, my friends helped me with a clever solution.

The morning glories in the widow's garden were the true sign that September was here. The little blue-purple flowers were spreading and growing anywhere they could. The roses were also in bloom, which indicated that it was not a hot September in El Paso. The nights were cool and the windows of the two-story apartments were open all day. School started and my English was not as good as it had been when school let out in May. During the summer, I lost some of my English vocabulary because I didn't use it. I had only been back in school two weeks and the teacher and I had already gone around and around about my speaking Spanish.

"English is spoken in school…even when you are speaking to your friends, young lady!" the teacher snapped when she eavesdropped on a conversation I was having in the closet of our classroom. I had just commented to Raquel that I wished I could get a new coat this winter just like the one she had last year. The teacher appeared from nowhere and caught us speaking Spanish. So, Raquel and I had to each stand in a corner of that stupid closet during recess. You may as well have put me in front of the firing squad because it hurt just as much to miss recess. "¡*Dísparen*, fire!" said the teacher *commendante,* in my fantasy. "Only English in spoken in school, in El Paso, in Texas and in America, *entiendes*, do you understand?

My pledge of allegiance had already earned me a note home to my father. In the note, Palm was informed that my version of the pledge was a mockery. How was it possible that he could not teach me such a small task? Would he or his wife please teach me the pledge? The note said, "Gloria enjoys the laughter and disruption she causes each morning." Palm smiled when he read the part about Carmen teaching me the pledge.

"Gloria, let me hear the pledge." He wanted to hear for himself what the problem was. Palm listened with interest and smiled a couple of times. When I was finished he put on a serious face and talked to me about my presentation.

"You mix the words around…you move the words in your pledge." Then seeing the puzzled look on my face, he said, "You take a word out and put the wrong once in its place." He struggled to explain. "You don't know what you are saying. Didn't the teacher explain?"

"I guess that she did …but I didn't understand her Chinese." I replied, trying to be clever. "You explain it to me."

"Stop clowning! And stop calling English Chinese. You're not funny anymore," he said annoyed. It took a long time but he tried to explain what each of the words meant and in what order they went. But each time I tried to say the pledge I would make new revisions. I couldn't get it right.

"I will give you a *tostón*, a walking Liberty fifty cent piece, if you learn it by your birthday. That gives you a week. Practice saying it with your friends and you will get the fifty-cent piece." He knew that I loved the walking lady silver coin because I loved what it could buy. That would encourage me to learn the pledge. For that much money, I agreed immediately. I started thinking of how I would spend the money. My dreams were filled full of fifty-cent pieces that night: beautiful silver ladies dancing with the stars all around.

The next day, I met the boys at the jalopy. I told them what the teacher had done and what Palm had promised me if I learned the pledge. They were impressed with the money. We quickly made plans on how to spend it. It could easily buy us all *raspadas*, ice cones, and some gum. Or it could pay for all of us to go to the movies on the Saturday after my birthday. It was endless, what we could do with fifty cents.

Then my brother Carlos, who was the oldest and a fourth grader, reminded me that I had to recite the pledge correctly in order to get the money. We all agreed that it was a problem since I didn't understand the words. So each of them proceeded to recite the pledge slowly and carefully, right in my face. They put a great deal of acting into the words. Still I didn't say it correctly any of the times I tried.

"I guess you want to put me in front of the firing squad just like the teacher would like to," I said, explaining my fantasy to them. They liked the idea and said why didn't we take the time to play the scene. They would shoot me down if I didn't learn the words.

Carlos and I went home to get broomsticks and hats. Flaco was to get a handkerchief to put across my eyes. Pelón was to bring back his cowboy holster for Carlos, the *commendante*. We agreed to meet after lunch. I hoped Carmen had something good for us because all that pledging made me hungry.

After lunch we gathered at the jalopy. Carlos was in charge. The other boys were the soldiers who helped me learn and they were also the members of the firing squad. It was agreed that we would break the pledge into parts. As soon as I learned a part, we would move on to the next part. They were very relieved when they discovered that I had no problem with the first part.

"I pledge allegiance…," I began well. "To the republic…"

"No…No! To the flag…the *bandera*, Yoya! Flaco would yell. "*A la pared*, to the wall." We walked over to the jalopy. I stood in front of it. Prieto put the handkerchief around my eyes and said a prayer for me with his head bowed.

"That's not necessary!" barked Carlos as he yelled for the men to ready themselves. "Shoot! *A toda ametralladora*, like a machine gun."

"We only have rifles, Commander," Flaco yelled sharply.

The rest of the afternoon went like that. Each time I made a mistake, I faced the firing squad. It was a lot of fun. By the time the sky started to turn the color of a Sinaloa mango, I had thoroughly exhausted the group. I didn't want to play anymore. Let Palm keep his *tostón*. But the boys said we would try again the next day. Carlos would think about the problem.

"Palm said you have to learn it by your birthday?" asked Flaco. "When is that?"

"In a week, I think," I answered. "It's September the 12th. Pretty soon, no?" Carlos nodded yes.

"Are you having a party?" asked Prieto.

"I have never had a party. Not that I know of," I said.

"Don't you want one? A party with a *piñata*," Carlos added. "We can ask Palm."

"Yes, but I don't think I am going to have one," I said sadly. "It would be nice. Don't people bring gifts?"

"Yes, let's plan a party. We'll make invitations and take them to the neighbors," Flaco said excited by the idea. "Palm will have to give you a party?"

"Yes, *cómo que nó*? He got a new wife and a new car. He can give me a party," I said bravely. "And we'll tell everyone to bring a present. No gift…don't come!"

The next day we met at the jalopy. No one could find any paper to make the invitations, so we simply went to all the neighbors' houses and invited them in person. Flaco was in charge of telling them to bring a present. I felt it might be *falta de educación*, lacking manners, for me to say it. Then we agreed that I had to tell Palm that evening. I became a little uncomfortable with that idea. But who cares, that's how he told me he had a new wife and a new car.

We got back to the problem of the pledge. Once again, we set up our scene. Carlos encouraged me with whispers and yelled at me when I missed. The rest of them loved it when they had to execute me.

"Young lady, that is not right!" Carlos would imitate his teacher. "Now, say it after me. Indivisible is what you should say, not invisible. Invisible means you can't see, Yoya!" Then he gave up. "Let me explain it to you in Spanish, but you must say it in English. Spanish will not be right." Soon, we stopped the play and talked about the party until I saw Palm coming home. Carlos and I turned to meet him.

"Tomorrow we'll sing the pledge…for sure you'll learn it then," said Pelón. He was inspired by the idea as he went off singing the pledge to play with Flaco in his apartment.

After dinner, Palm and I were sitting in the living room while Carmen was cleaning the dishes. Palm took out a pack of cigarettes that he had bought at the store. Carmen didn't like the smell of the ones we made so he bought Lucky Strikes just to please her. They were so fat and smooth, unlike the homemade ones. And she didn't let him fix his one drink anymore. He didn't complain. She certainly had changed things.

Palm asked me how my pledge was coming along. I told him about the game the boys and I had made of it. He smiled as he always did when I would tell him about our plays. He explained the word indivisible with the box of cigarettes he had just opened. And he explained the word invisible by telling me it was like ghosts I saw that no one else saw. I softly hit his arm for saying that, but I finally understood. When he asked me to recite the pledge to see if I learned it, I refused. I told him I wanted to surprise him for my birthday. And speaking of my birthday, the boys thought it would be nice if I had a party. We invited the neighbors today. What did he think?

"A party, Yoya! Whose idea was that?" He muttered some nasty words under his breath. "I don't have the money for a party. Where am I going to get the money?"

"You had the money for the car. All we need to have is a piñata, candy for the piñata, a cake and some Velvet ice cream. The big people will want some *cerveza*. I will ask López to bring some from Juárez. Everyone will be happy. Especially me." I tried to solve the problem. When Palm didn't answer, I continued to give him ideas as to where to get things for the party. "The cake can be bought at the bakery at the corner from you. López can bring the piñata from Juárez.

The poor man couldn't answer. Then Carmen came into the living room. She saw how Palm looked and asked what was the matter. I didn't really want to tell her, but I didn't know what to do about my father's long face. So I told her about the party. She started laughing, something I had never seen before. It made her seem real. She told Palm what a clever child I was. She said that she had always felt bad because she didn't have a party until she was eight. Her family and some friends in Juárez could bring the cake. Carmen's excitement lifted my father's spirits. I was grateful for that, but at the same time I was surprised. He laughed. After a while, he said that since I had already told the neighbors and since Carmen was so happy to give the party, that it would be all right. He just didn't like parties that he couldn't afford.

"Your birthday is in a week, but we can't have it then because it is a Wednesday. We'll have to wait until Saturday, September 15. That is also the night before Mexican Independence. You remember how many people were in the neighborhood last year? he groaned. "Now for sure I know I can't afford it."

I started thinking about the year before. The terrible thing that happened to Luisito in Juárez. I hadn't thought about it in months. It seemed like it was so long ago that we went to sit with his family. I wondered if Señora Olga would join us in the backyard. It was ten days until my first birthday party. It seemed like a long time.

The next day at the jalopy, the boys and I tried singing the pledge and making each of the boys represent one of the words that I couldn't get. Pelón had a small flag that his rich cousins had given him when he went to visit them on the 4th of July. The boys formed a line that represented the flag, republic, nation, liberty and justice. The flag was in Pelón's hand and he was also the republic. Flaco was one nation and indivisible. Prieto was liberty and justice. Pelón was the first, then Flaco and then Prieto. All I had to remember was the order of the boys by their age. Carlos, the commander, was in charge and the one who thought of the idea. By the second time, I could say it without any mistakes. I jumped around and fought an invisible boxer just like the Brown Bomber did. Then we started planning how we would spend the money.

On Sunday, the widow came over and talked to Palm. She told him that Eduardo was coming home next week and the rest of the neighbors wanted to help with my party and get together with the boys home from the war. She said the whole neighborhood wanted to do the midnight cry that begins Mexican Independence. Everyone was going to pitch in with the grownup part of the party after Yoya and the children had their piñata. Palm was relieved and thanked her for her help.

I was so excited for the next couple of days. The teacher was happy I could recite the pledge and I had stopped clowning around. On my birthday that Wednesday, I said the pledge for Palm and he was proud of me. He gave me the fifty cent piece. I also said it for López, who did not speak English. He kissed me and said I looked pretty saying it. Because I wanted Carmen to make me a good party, I was on my best behavior. Friday afternoon, the boys and I bought *raspadas* and gum with my money. On Friday night, I went to sleep wondering if Señora Olga and Señora Alma would be at the party. The two women detested war; no medals made up for their losses. Only the widow's son came back without any wounds.

NOTE

[1] This chapter is reprinted from López-Stafford, G. (1996). *A place in El Paso: A Mexican-American childhood.* Santa Fe, NM: University of New Mexico Press.

P. Frank, El Centro Maya Guatemalteco

In April 2015, Jupiter suffered a setback in its remarkable recent history of confronting classism, racism and contempt for the outcast poor.

A town that once set a high bar for others by founding at El Sol its workers' community center, was shocked at the exposure of a canker still alive in its heart. Not only members of the horrified families, but its civic institutions, centers of formation such as churches, schools, scouts, fraternal associations, we were required to ask how their community had nurtured such disease at its core? How were teens among us lost to such evil?

First instinct in such dreadfulness is to disown, judge and punish rather than to grapple with our part in the repugnant reality. We do not share our young people's aversion and disdain for the workers, do we? From whom did they learn contempt for life?

What is it about our structuring of our communities that could have formed them without a sense of respect for others, the "Guates". How did we effectively leave our progeny bereft of a sense of reverence?

Listening to our dialogue, one can't help but be struck by the poverty of response in local media. For news, Baltimore eclipsed Jupiter. El Sol, if one were to believe the PB Post responded with something like "Our workers will pass the hat for the bereaved family." That does not do justice to the agency which walks a narrow line as it moves to fundraising from unpopular advocacy but it questions whether community institutions can leave their burden any longer of social formation to today's El Sol.

As Jupiter sets out to recapture the lovely direction of a few years ago, it will be important the community learn of the Sunday hermeneutic reflections in the churches, the presentations at fraternal associations and above all, the engagement of school teachers and counselors with the tragic crisis of our children.

Spanish Spanish Translation/Traducion Español por Padre Frank, the Guatemalan Maya Center

En el mes de abril la ciudad de Júpiter sufrió un terrible retroceso en sus esfuerzos de combatir las divisiones de clases, el racismo, y el desprecio por los pobres marginados. Una ciudad que se ha distinguido como ejemplo al fundar El Sol, el centro comunitario para trabajadores, fue entristecida al exponerse una úlcera que persiste.

No solamente familias horrorizadas, pero instituciones cívicas, centros de formación como iglesias, el sistema escolar, asociaciones fraternales, etc., tuvieron que preguntarse como su comunidad había permitido que se desarrollara esta malignidad en su medio. ¿Cómo fue posible que estos jóvenes pudieran participar en estas acciones viles? Nuestro primer instinto en una tragedia como ésta es negar, juzgar, y castigar, en vez de confrontar la situación y nuestra parte en esta repugnante realidad.

¿Compartimos la aversión y desdeño de nuestra gente joven por los trabajadores? ¿De quién aprendieron este desprecio por la vida humana? *¿Qué hicimos al formar nuestras comunidades que nuestros jóvenes han podido ser criados sin un sentido de respeto para otros, para los "guates". ¿Cómo fue posible que dejáramos a nuestros jóvenes sin un sentido de reverencia?*

Al escuchar nuestro diálogo no nos queda más remedio que sorprendernos con la insignificante respuesta por parte de los medios de comunicaciones. Los noticieros de Palm Beach cubrieron mucho más las noticias de Baltimore que las locales. El Sol, según el Palm Beach Post, ha dicho que los trabajadores van a recolectar fondos para ayudar a la familia de la víctima. Pero nos preguntamos si la gente y las instituciones de la comunidad pueden seguir dejando el peso de la formación a un centro de obreros.

Mientras Júpiter trata de recapturar su distinguida dirección de hace unos años atrás, es importante que la comunidad se entere de las enseñanzas en las iglesias, de las presentaciones en las asociaciones fraternales, y sobre todo, la preparación de los maestros y consejeros en los colegios.

Figure 1. Fr. Frank O'Loughlin with Cesar Chavez 1974 (Fr. Frank O'Loughlin © 1974)

AVI CHOMSKY

3. A CENTRAL AMERICAN DRAMA IN FOUR ACTS

The Central American child migrant "crisis" of the summer of 2014 was shocking to Americans. On the surface, the stories of parent-child separation, of vulnerable children, of violence, seemed to inspire either a visceral response of pity or sympathy (we should help these poor children!), or a sense of frustration, victimization, and resentment (we have enough problems here, why do we have to help everyone in the world?). But in a deeper sense, I would like to argue, the situation was shocking because it jarringly challenged narratives and categories about immigration that have been instilled in us since elementary school. Even immigrants quickly absorb these narratives. In this chapter, I'd like to identify these narratives and challenge them, and explain how they have helped to blind us to the ways that U.S. immigration law has functioned in the past and continues to function today.

What historians would call the "master narrative" of immigration goes something like this. The United States is a country of immigrants. In the first act of the narrative, the new country was settled and then founded by immigrants seeking freedom and a better life. In the second act, in the nineteenth century, as the country industrialized, new waves of immigrants were welcomed at Ellis Island and went to work in the burgeoning factories. While the first immigrants had been primarily Anglo-Saxon and Protestant, the new waves came from Ireland and from Europe's southern and eastern peripheries (like Poland, Italy, Greece, and Russia) and included Jews, Catholics, and Orthodox Christians. In the third act, in the 1920s Congress imposed immigration quotas that severely limited this new immigration until finally—the fourth and final act of the drama–the Immigration Act of 1965 leveled the playing field again, prioritizing family reunion and needed skills, and allowing equal access to immigration for all of the world's countries. In the master narrative, immigration policy is domestic policy, and foreign policy is irrelevant.

While this narrative is not completely false, it is partial and skewed in a way that fundamentally distorts our understanding of this country's past and present. The narrative is biased in three ways: with respect to race, with respect to geography, and with respect to labor. Untangling these distortions helps us place the Central American migrant crisis in a very different context. The narrative tells us *one* story of immigration to the United States: a story of white people, migrating to the East Coast, and working in factories. It's a story of freedom, a story of industrialization

M. López-Stafford Levy (Ed.), Children from the Other America, 23–29.

and improving standards of living, and a story of assimilation and the melting pot. But that story has an underside that needs to be incorporated.

ACT I: WHITE COLONIZATION AND THE SEARCH FOR FREEDOM

The story usually begins facing west, as English migrants travel to America. But if we begin the story "facing east," we quickly see that there are "two faces of American freedom."[1] "Freedom" for English settlers was predicated on invading, expelling, expropriating, and slaughtering the prior inhabitants of the land. For America's Native inhabitants, these "settlers" were invaders. These migrants' "freedom" to acquire land entailed three centuries of dispossession, implemented by law and by violence. As American settlers and sovereignty extended southwards and westwards, Native American freedom was progressively circumscribed. By the time white America's domination of the continent was complete in the 1890s, Native American sovereignty had been crushed and the population reduced to scraps of unwanted territory deemed "reservations." The process of white migration, expansion, and freedom *could not exist without* Native American dispossession: they are intrinsically and irremediably part of the same story. The immigrant history of the United States begins with a physical and ideological erasure of Native American history.

The story of immigrants as people seeking freedom is a racialized story in another way as well. For large numbers of migrants to colonial America, migration entailed a loss of freedom rather than a search for freedom. Although Africans, like Europeans, voyaged to America, their experience was more akin to that of Native Americans: it was one of violence, brutality, and enslavement rather than one of freedom. Furthermore, the freedom experienced by Europeans in the Americas was based on the labor of increasing numbers of forced migrants from Africa. To enjoy the "freedom" of America, Europeans needed the land and the labor of others. Seen from the perspective of Africans, the obsession of white Europeans with their own "freedom," and the notion of the United States as a beacon of freedom, is more than a bit ironic. In fact, the independent United States retained the institution of slavery longer than did any European or Latin American land with the exception of Brazil and the Spanish colonies of Cuba and Puerto Rico. The story of the immigrant origins of the United States is necessarily a white history, one that deliberately erases the experiences of the victims of white freedom.

ACT II: FREEDOM AND A BETTER LIFE: THE WHITE STORY CONTINUES

By the mid-nineteenth century, the master narrative of migration changes to one of non-Anglo-Saxon (but still white) immigrants pouring into the now-independent United States seeking freedom and a better life, and finding work in the burgeoning industries of the northeast and eventually the midwest. First coming from French Canada, then Ireland, then southern and eastern Europe, they streamed into Ellis Island and were welcomed by the Statue of Liberty with its stirring words from the poem by Emma Lazarus: "Give me your tired, your poor, your huddled masses yearning to breathe free!"

"The basic idea of welcoming immigrants to our shores is central to our way of life, it is in our DNA," Barack Obama proclaimed on July 4, 2014, in the context of the Central American migrant crisis.[2] Surely he had in mind those immigrants who came to "our shores" across the Atlantic Ocean (rather than from the west across the Pacific Ocean, or from the south across the Caribbean or the Rio Grande); in fact he implies that these welcomed immigrants arrived by ship rather than by airplane or by raft, car, bus, or foot.

The welcoming of (white) immigrants in the nineteenth century was in part a racial project: one aimed at increasing the white population of the country while simultaneously expelling, deporting, and excluding non-whites. "Immigrants" were by definition white, because until 1870 only whites could become citizens—and after 1870, only whites and "people of African descent" could do so. Conveniently for the white racial project, the migration of "people of African descent" evaporated as the European trade in enslaved Africans drew to a close. For Africans, America represented enslavement, not freedom.

Conquest and expansion westward accompanied increased immigration in the nineteenth century. The Mexican American War (known to Mexicans as the War of the North American Invasion) brought half of Mexico's territory into the United States, and the end of nineteenth century saw the invasion of the west and the savage attacks against the remaining autonomous indigenous peoples there. Mexican citizens (though not the Native Americans in the territory) were theoretically offered US citizenship through the Treaty of Guadalupe Hidalgo, though a combination of federal, state, and territorial legislation and regulation soon imposed qualifications that denied citizenship itself or at least its economic and political rights to those Mexicans not deemed to be white.[3]

Until the Civil War, there were few restrictions on entry into the United States. Racial exclusivity was maintained by restrictions on *citizenship* rather than on migration. White migrants were, in the words of Hiroshi Motomura, "intending citizens," and granted extensive rights to political and economic participation, including in many cases the right to vote. Those not defined as white—including Asians, Mexicans, Africans, and Native Americans—were excluded from those same rights through their exclusion from citizenship by virtue of their racial status.[4]

The implementation of citizenship by birth with the Fourteenth Amendment in 1868 drastically altered the ways that Congress dealt with immigration. No longer could white supremacy be maintained by racially-exclusive citizenship, because now anybody (except Native Americans, who were explicitly excluded from the right to citizenship by birth) born in the United States was automatically a citizen. Racial restrictions on immigration quickly followed, with prohibitions increasing until by 1917 some three-quarters of the planet's territory had been defined as "Asia" and included in the "Asiatic barred zone." Peoples from "Asia" were racially ineligible to citizenship, and thus necessarily prohibited from immigrating.[5] Thus while the Statue of Liberty was welcoming (European) immigrants on the east coast of the United States in 1886, non-Europeans were being increasingly restricted from entering the country.

ACT III: RESTRICTING IMMIGRANTS—BUT NOT MEXICANS

While Chinese (and other Asian) exclusion is generally incorporated as a footnote to U.S. immigration history, the national origins restrictions of 1921 and 1924 that limited *European* immigration are offered as a central—though aberrant—theme. Clearly, when boosters pronounce that the country has "always" welcomed immigrants, they are downplaying both the long history of racial exclusion, as well as the shorter period during which even European immigration was severely restricted.[6]

Despite the increasing racial and numerical restrictions on immigration, however, the southern border of the United States remained almost completely open. Western Hemisphere countries (which in practice meant Mexico), had no numerical restrictions placed on them. Mexican migrant workers played a growing role in the railroad, mining, and agricultural industries of the west and southwest, and as Chinese and other Asian migrants were excluded, Mexican labor became even more essential. When the U.S. Border Patrol was created in 1924 and deployed on the country's southern frontier, its main purpose was to prevent *Chinese* migrants from entering the country undetected. In the eyes of Congress, Mexicans were not "immigrants" or intending citizens, but rather workers. Their labor was indispensable, and they could be conveniently shipped back across the border if they became unnecessary—or if they became too demanding. The massive deportations of the 1930s and Operation Wetback in 1954, and the Bracero Program that brought hundreds of thousands of Mexicans on temporary contracts every year from 1942 to 1964 (not fully ended until 1967), illustrate this opportunistic use of Mexican labor outside of the parameters of immigration and citizenship.

Immigration law, then, was written not written for Mexicans. It was written to welcome Europeans, and exclude Asians—and ignore Mexicans. Until 1965.

ACT IV: IMMIGRATION REFORM AND FOREIGN POLICY

The Hart-Celler Act of 1965 (also known as the Immigration and Nationality Act of 1965) implemented a major overhaul of the immigration system. It is best known for replacing the national origins quotas and racial restrictions with equal quotas for each of the world's countries, and for setting up a preference system based on family relations and jobs skills. Less well known is the fact that Western Hemisphere immigration was restricted for the first time. Ignoring the century-old patterns of labor recruitment and migration that had linked the southern and western United States with Mexico, the generations of Mexicans who had incorporated patterns of circular migration into their regions' economies, and the employers who relied on this labor, especially to fill California's seasonal agricultural labor needs, a cap of 20,000 "immigrants" a year was placed on Mexico. The Bracero Program was simultaneously phased out, leaving workers and employers with only one alternative: illegality. Today somewhere between 50 and 90% of California's seasonal farm laborers are undocumented.

Congress had treated Mexican workers differently from "immigrants" (that is, Europeans who were intending citizens) for many decades. The legislated system of the Bracero Program, and the system of illegality that replaced it, were premised on the idea that Mexican migrants were young, male, seasonal workers.

But things changed in the 1980s and 1990s. On one hand, the migrant stream changed. On the other, American attitudes and policies towards "illegality" and towards immigrants in general, shifted towards the nativist end of a spectrum that has swung back and forth numerous times over the decades. The two phenomena were not unrelated.

U.S. military and economic involvement in Central America dates back to the end of the nineteenth century, when the United Fruit Company established plantations on the Caribbean coasts of the region and the U.S. government took it upon itself to ensure a favorable climate for U.S. business in the region—by military means if necessary. During the period of "dollar diplomacy" during the 1910s and 20s, the United States established long-term occupations in Haiti, the Dominican Republic, and Nicaragua, with shorter interventions in Cuba and Honduras.[7] With a dreary predictability, these interventions set the stage for lengthy military dictatorships, and left most of each country's productive land in the hands of a small group of elites or American companies.

Since World War II, the United States has made it clear that reforms to this system or attempts to redistribute the wealth or privilege the interests of the population over those of foreign investors would not be tolerated. A new wave of foreign investment, first in non-traditional agricultural enterprises like cotton and cattle, and then in the *maquiladora* industry, sparked new movements for social change. From the overthrow of Guatemala's democratically elected reformist president Jacobo Arbenz in 1954, to the "Contra" war against Nicaragua's revolutionary Sandinista government in the 1980s and the coup against Honduras's democratically elected and reformist president Manuel Zelaya in 2009, the United States continued to be deeply involved, economically and militarily, in Central America's affairs.

Increasing U.S. involvement in the civil wars of Central America in the 1980s—in particular in support of the right-wing governments Guatemala and El Salvador–militarized society and created tens of thousands of refugees, some of whom fled across borders and into the United States. The peace agreements of the 1990s set the stage for neoliberal economic reforms and the Central America Free Trade Agreement, which only exacerbated poverty, unemployment, and inequality. Once the refugees of the 1980s had become the pioneers and paved the way, new generations of migrants followed them.

In Mexico too, neoliberal reforms and the 1994 NAFTA both strengthened already-tight ties with the United States, and created new sectors of dispossessed people, especially indigenous people in the rural south, who soon entered the migrant stream. In the United States, the 1986 Immigration Reform and Control Act offered legal status to significant numbers of undocumented immigrants—but also imposed harsh "enforcement" measures and set the stage for an anti-immigrant backlash. Like twenty-first century proposals for comprehensive immigration reform, IRCA proposed to resolve the "problem" of illegality by granting legal status to some, and persecuting or eliminating others.

The false logic—that offering full rights to some migrants should be counterbalanced by increased discrimination against others—caught on among nativist circles and opportunistic media and political figures, who began to clamor for the country to increase deportations and seal the border. But every measure to further militarize and obstruct the border seemed to result in a growth, rather than a reduction, in the numbers of undocumented people in the United States. As it became more difficult and dangerous to cross the border, more and more migrants decided to stay, rather than return home.[8] The undocumented population diversified and grew. In a vicious cycle, so did the push to demonize them and "secure" the border.[9]

CENTRAL AMERICAN CHILDREN

The crisis in the summer of 2014 grew out of a long history. Or rather, out of several interrelated long histories. One is the history of US immigration law, elaborated over several hundred years to privilege white citizenship while catering to employers' demand for cheap, exploitable Mexican workers. "Illegality" was a twentieth-century concept constructed to justify the exploitation of Mexican workers, and it gained prominence in the late twentieth century as other, more explicitly racist rationales lost favor.

A second history is that of U.S. relations with Mexico and Central America, which have likewise aimed at offering U.S. businesses a favorable investment climate there. This has meant that nationalist and redistributive policies, and the governments that implement them, have been toppled, while governments were encouraged or coerced into offering economic incentives to foreign investors. Attempts to challenge these policies were brutally repressed. That parents would flee to the United States, in hopes of providing food, shelter, health care, and education for their children, is not surprising. Nor is it surprising that some of those children would follow their parents to the promised land.

Pundits and policymakers found themselves perplexed, in the summer of 2014, at how to respond to the influx of Central American youth. Their very presence undermined the comforting myths and narratives that we as a country have constructed about the history of U.S. immigration and foreign policy. Yet if we do not confront these myths, the presence and actions of these youth will remain a mystery, and the nature of the crisis obscured. The real crisis is how deliberate policies enacted by the most powerful country in the world have created dispossession and desperation among its closest neighbors. Until we are able to acknowledge and understand the past, we will not be able to act in the present for a better future.

NOTES

[1] Daniel K. Richter, *Facing East from Indian Country: A Native History of Early America* (Harvard University Press, 2001); Aziz Rana, *Two Faces of American Freedom* (Harvard University Press, 2010).

[2] Steve Holland, "Obama: 'Our Immigration System is Broken,'" *Business Insider*, July 4, 2014. http://www.businessinsider.com/r-on-july-fourth-holiday-obama-urges-immigration-overhaul-2014-04.

[3] See Marta Menchaca, *Naturalizing Mexican Immigrants: A Texas History* (University of Texas Press, 2011), especially chapter 1.

[4] Hiroshi Motomura, *Americans in Waiting: The Lost Story of Immigration and Citizenship in the United States* (Oxford University Press, 2006).

[5] See Mae Ngai, *Impossible Subjects: Illegal Aliens and the Making of Modern America* (Princeton University Press, 2004).

[6] Barack Obama, "Address to the Nation on Immigration," November 14, 2014. https://www.whitehouse.gov/the-press-office/2014/11/20/remarks-president-address-nation-immigration

[7] See, among many others, Paul Dosal, *Doing Business with the Dictators: A Political History of United Fruit in Guatemala, 1899–1944* (Scholarly Resources, 1993); Jason M. Colby, *The Business of Empire: United Fruit, Race, and U.S. Expansion in Central America* (Cornell University Press, 2011); Walter LaFeber, *Inevitable Revolutions: The United States in Central America* (W. W. Norton & Co., 2nd 3d. 1993).

[8] Jorge Durand and Douglas S. Massey, "What We Learned from the Mexican Migration Project," in Jorge Durand and Douglas S. Massey, eds., *Crossing the Border: Research from the Mexican Migration Project* (Russell Sage Foundation, 2006), 11–12.

[9] See for example HR 399, the "Secure Our Borders First Act," introduced in the House of Representatives in January 2015. https://www.congress.gov/bill/114th-congress/house-bill/399

FLSST@yahoogroups.com
Sent: Monday, December 01, 2014
To: flsst@yahoogroups.com

I just wanted to share this little anecdote with you all; I wasn't sure how to react and therefore I seek the wisdom of others.

The 9th grade ELL class today was fairly badly-behaved, which is the daily norm; with half of them out of their seats, laughing, loud talking, and rough playing going on. There is an unusual amount of horseplay and physical mock-fighting among the Guatemalan students who are newcomers/beginners in English language, which physical playing we school personnel are all getting very tired of, as it is December, and they've been roughhousing and punching each other every hour of every day in school since August. Let's just say, a lot more teachers are writing discipline referrals and our collective patience and our "compassionate waiting time while cultural and academic adjustment occur" seem to have simultaneously come to an end among the school staff. Bottom line, it's a secondary school and we are tired of rough, out-of-seats horseplay every hour of every school-day. Cultural differences and prior schooling differences or not, we are tired of it by now.

In the hallway during the "passing time" from one class period to the next, an older bilingual Mexican-American boy, R., a great kid, 11th grader, came by my room to see if I could give him a Band-Aid. Of course I can. And then I said, "R., I wish you had come here earlier, you could have helped me with the freshmen ESOL class, they were mostly all out of their seats and playing and roughhousing again." (I know that R. speaks perfect Spanish. I was intimating that he could have translated for me to the class. He knew what I meant.)

And R. replied, "NO, Miss, I won't help you with that. I don't want to see it. I see enough of their behavior in my own Biology class. I am sick and tired of their behavior. It disgusts me. As a Latino myself [and he repeated this part in Spanish then, "Como Latino…"], I don't want to be associated with that behavior. I don't want people to think that is how all Latinos behave, that we don't know how to control ourselves and act more or less grown-up in high school, that we just play and talk and laugh all the time. I don't want to witness any more of it than I already have to. I'm sorry but I just can't see it, I can't stand it. I really really can't stand it. I can't help you with that class."

Obviously R. was vehement. I completely understood his reaction, and I sympathize with where he is coming from on that, but I did not know what to say back to him. I guess I could have reassured him that most people have sense enough to distinguish people person by person and not put everyone from one ethnicity in the same boat … not that I really believe that most people (John Q. Public) really DO have this good sense. But I guess I should have said something in reply.

Behavior-wise on the newcomer-Guatemalan-males front, we have dragged in every available resource to speak to the kids and to their parents about school behavior and appropriateness. Older kids who can translate talk to the younger newcomers all the time about "This is a secondary school and you can't act that way here" themes. The male guidance counselor who speaks Spanish has had serious talks with them. The parents have had an ESOL Parents' Night where we got a huge crowd (155 people) and we talked about grades and behavior and other expectations in a FL public high school. We talk to kids' parents individually on the phone too. We also use 'Parentlink', which is an automatic system making calls to parents for us with messages in Spanish from a menu of 75 messages. We write referrals and send kids out to ISS with Security. Heck, I have even had the bilingual Mexican kitchen-manager in my classroom to speak to the kids! (He happens to be a former ESOL student of mine from a long time ago, in fact, but still, it's not every year that I drag in the kitchen manager to speak to kids!)

Any advice on either front, folks? I'd appreciate it.

Thanks
Mercedes

BENTON FAZZOLARI

4. REFLECTIONS ON THE IMAGE OF IMMIGRANT MINORS FROM CENTRAL AMERICA

APPEARANCE

Were it not for appearances, the world would be a perfect crime, that is, a crime without a criminal, without a victim and without a motive. And the truth would forever have withdrawn from it and its secret would never be revealed, for want of any clues [traces] being left behind. (Jean Baudrillard)

In his book *The Image: A Guide to Pseudo-Events in America*, Boorstin (1962/1992) tells us that there are two types of events: the "pseudo-event" and the "spontaneous event." The pseudo-event does not leave behind appearances. Everything disappears. It manufactures perfection. It produces assumptions and molds them into "facts." It frames and narrows. It closes and confines. All of its variables and contradictions arrange symmetrically and systematically. It is logical. It begins and ends simultaneously. It disappears. It is pure non-appearance. Everything within the pseudo-event lives within a pre-determined outline. It is all-inclusive. It creates discursive absence. It is violent and obscene in its dissolution of dialogue. It is the perversion of enquiry. It pollutes and degenerates its own moment. It is not propaganda, but rather a steel box full of everything and of which, nothing can enter. Propaganda is honest and obvious. The pseudo-event deceives, distorts, generates, and disintegrates. The entire globe resides in the pseudo-event.

The spontaneous event is pure appearance. It reveals amidst a rampant and hysterical delivery of (pre)structured pseudo-events. It is not produced and answers no questions. Or its production remains uncertain. It requires discourse. It breeds enquiry. It necessitates investigation. It carries nothing predetermined. It is open. It is ours. It is a moment of freely ignited discomfort, outrage, and ecstasy. It is not arranged or processed. It is what is left behind to be placed in front.

The flood of unaccompanied minors to the United States border exemplifies the spontaneous event or that of an appearance. The existence of tens of thousands of children in the "processing center" in objective/concrete reality is simply the appearance of something left behind at the crime scene. The perfect crime will leave no appearances. The unaccompanied minors represent the evidence of past pseudo-events (crimes). The recognition of this appearance serves to identify the manufactured pseudo-events of the past. This reconstructive process or this process

M. López-Stafford Levy (Ed.), Children from the Other America, 33–48.

to properly (honestly) pinpoint, with accuracy, the perplexing intersections of economic, political, and social variables stands as a formidable task. This task is overshadowed by a more important consideration: how do we prevent the appearance of the unaccompanied minors from becoming a pseudo-event? Is it possible?

THE PERFECT CRIME

The pseudo-event is the perfect crime. Debord (1967/1994) asserts that "images chosen and constructed by someone else have everywhere become the individual's principle connection to the world" (p. 12). The pseudo-event as a "synthetic happening arranged or instigated to advertise something, to sell something, to influence public opinion … [is] image generated" (Rich, 2008, p. 80). The perfect crime disappears because its image is dominant and without appearances is untraceable. The perfect crime is the disappearance of American Foreign Policy in Central America as a pseudo-event. Furthermore, if all images related to the United States intervention in Central America are constructed as monopoly for the consumption of the American population then the entire history and the entire perception of the happening(s) and history of the happening(s) exists as crime which implodes into meaninglessness. James North (2014) writes, "Americans, especially young Americans, do not know about how their own government funded murderous right-wing dictatorships in Central America back in the 1980s" (p. 1). North is only half correct. Central America is itself a pseudo-event (as well as a continent). This means that any image of Central America is framed by "someone else" for consumption. North's article is from *The Nation*, a journal that manufactures pseudo-events.

North is certainly correct, as is widely known, that the United States funded murderous dictatorships. But the significant factor rests in the fact that events disappear in the context of image driven construction, particularly when the images are primarily broadcast by the elite sectors of media power. Regardless, the mirroring of elite image projections of events, by alternate sources, through the filtering of the same specific mediums (television, web journals, social networks, etc.) dissolves the event into the unreality of the pseudo-event. The mediums are receptacles of alteration. They house and then project. The projections overwhelm the essence of the spontaneous. Spontaneous events cannot subsist inside the medium's receptacle.

The image of unaccompanied minors becomes a constructed commodity sold as an event, but in reality is simply Boorstin's "pseudo-event." Debord (1990) mentions, "Each and every new product is supposed to offer a dramatic shortcut to the long awaited promised land of total consumption. As such it is ceremoniously presented as the unique and ultimate product" (p. 20). Within the mediums, the event, in its silent capitulation is a product and is perceived as a product to be consumed. Consumption does not inspire action as the act of consuming *is* the (in)action of image production. Appearances do not hide; they are hidden by mediums. Once the appearance is consumed it can only become waste. The perfect crime is committed when the appearance of unaccompanied minors is commodified and disposed of within and by the mediums of power. The only possible appearances are personal and independent of or in resistance to power.

The image is accompanied by myth construction. Roland Barthes (1957/2012) describes the impact associated with an image from popular media of the beheading of Guatemalan Communists (p. 116). He paraphrases Serreau who asserts that "we are looking at it from inside our freedom" (p. 116). With a perspective that begins in freedom, as opposed to the oppression of Guatemala, the image does not allow experience. Instead the image implies that "Someone shuddered for us, reflected for us, [and] judged for us" (p. 116). By the time the image enters public consciousness through media, it is a final product. Further, a caption or commentary of the image equally dissolves the meaning of the image into a single (or perhaps dual) meaning. Baudrillard (1981/1994) concludes that "The loss of meaning is directly linked to the dissolving, dissuasive action of information, the media, and the mass media" (p. 79). Clearly, meaning dissolves into a substance of myth. But myths are powerful.

The myth saturates the image. In this saturation, the essence of the all-inclusive nature of the produced and consumed image appears. But it loses color. It lacks the necessary energy for reprisal. Baudrillard (1981/1994) continues, "Myth exists, but one must guard against thinking that people believe in it" (p. 81). The final product that myth creates can only be absorbed. It cannot involve reflection of action. This is true because it *cannot* be believed, only accepted. This significant distinction centers the basic assumptions located in the image of the Central America immigrant minors. Their information through image and possibly text lacks meaning because the medium lacks the ability to generate meaning. The meaning implodes. The myth lives but is only myth, which is unbelievable. The masses who view the image run on inertia.

Perhaps the overwhelming presence of media images with text (pseudo-events/ myths) generates the ambivalence of the masses. The media does not create awareness of the political and social consequences of an event, but rather serves the opposite purpose. This is possible. Baudrillard (1981/1994) asks, "Is it the masses who victoriously resist the media by directing or absorbing all the messages that the media produce without responding to them?" (p. 84). This paradox leaves the insertion of the immigrant minors into the machinery of the mass media complicated. Are the masses silent because of the function of information mediums? Is it inherent in the process of these mediums that the masses will ignore the information? For instance, will the masses respond to a news report that examines the immigrant minor population at the border?

Essentially, the meaning implodes through the mass media. It may be an act of unconscious rebellion on the part of the masses to simply receive pseudo-events or myths without a response. But a more accurate explanation is that they can do nothing to the contrary. The mediums (television, internet journals/videos, social media) not only require mass ambivalence, but create the nihilistic response. The simulation of events realizes mandatory unconscious nihilism. "All of us have entered live into simulation, into the ... indifferent, sphere of deterrence: in a bizarre fashion, nihilism has been entirely realized no longer through destruction, but through simulation and deterrence" (Baudrillard, 1994, p. 159). The entrance of images (simulation) through electronic media deters involvement. The masses must desorb information.

Misinformation or censorship no longer applies as a valid explanation for the disappearance of events. For example, Project Censorship (2015) is a group who claims on their website to "expose and oppose news censorship and ... promote independent investigative journalism, media literacy, and critical thinking." Certainly their work is admirable. Unfortunately, it mirrors and subsequently perpetuates the implosion of meaning or the creation of the pseudo-event (myth). By offering itself up as an alternative to mainstream media, but employing the same strategies of event production and consumption as the power media, it delegitimizes its own theses. Embedded firmly in the concept of democracy and progressive liberalism, it merely reproduces power in the form of a false dichotomy/binary. In simple terms, it cancels out and is canceled out by its own methods and mediums.

To be more specific, Project Censorship reaffirms that mass media produces meaning and influences people. This (re)affirmation leaves power relations intact. What results (or remains) is a battle of distant media entities broadcasting on the same mediums. The counter arguments dissolve each other simultaneously. The many news stories that pertain to environmental concerns, for example, are swallowed by the process of mass production and consumption. Embedded in environmental event reporting is environmental assumptions retained in the mediums of reportage. Project Censorship misses the absurd moment in de-censoring the obscenity of plastic collecting in the middle of the Pacific through the computer based mediums. Aside from the fact that computers are plastic, the internet image medium shapes mass distance as a consumable/ingestible production.

Noam Chomsky's theory of the media filter and agenda setters correctly identifies how power functions in media, but ignores the mediums of mass media. Chomsky's thesis of concision rightly identifies imposed limits on television. In *Manufacturing Consent* he mentions that "[News shows] like Nightline, McNeil/Lehrer and so on, if they were better propagandists, they would let dissidents on (Achbard & Wintonick, 1992). Let them on more, in fact. The reason is that they *would* sound like they are from Neptune." This intriguing statement applies not only to the inability of the radical to properly explain something due to the limits of concision, but also that the medium of television conflicts with, or more accurately, dissolves radicalism. Marshall McLuhan (1967) puts this into perspective when he said that the Vietnam War is a hot event broadcast on a cool medium. In basic terms, the content cannot maintain appearance on the medium. This leaves the content in a secondary placement.

McLuhan is right in his statement, but not because Vietnam was too hot (war as medium), but because the pseudo-event of Vietnam involved the coolness of participation in non-mediums or spontaneous appearances (the draft, anti-war conflict in the family, wounded/dead returning to the neighborhood). Vietnam could not easily dissolve on the medium because the medium of war held direct involvement with concrete reality. Conversely, The Gulf War was total spectacle/ pseudo (it did not take place) while The Iraq War maintains disappearance through distance and image. The fundamental point is that the border crossing of Central American immigrant minors contains a level of cool participation outside of the implosive media (teachers, social workers, sponsors, etc.). This specific moment of participation must be located as the centerpiece of involvement.

To further illustrate, Barthes (1957/2012) elucidates the function of the myth as simulation and modes of deterrence. He provides the example taken from a 1955 issue of *Paris-Match* of a seven year old blond boy named Bichon who is among the natives of Africa in the "Country of the Red Negroes" (p. 67). According to Barthes, this article "reveal[s] the Black world through the eyes of the white child" and "everything looks like a puppet show" (p. 68). Barthes continues, "The Black has no full or autonomous life; he is a peculiar, a bizarre object, reduced to parasitical function, which is to divert the white man by his vaguely threatening baroque: Africa is a more or less dangerous puppet show" (p. 68). Essentially, Central American immigrant minors disseminated through the image become myth. Their myth eludes a concrete center. When one views the long journey through the desert or the crowded detainment centers, it is mythology, a pseudo-event, a simulation, a spectacle and a deterrence. Like a seven month old child, who sees only through his own glazed expression and experience, the North American perceiver of the image cannot see otherwise. The image itself creates the myth as a medium. The myth remains firm in its singularity of detail.

From April of 2014 to July of 2015 countless articles and videos from countless sources reported the immigrant "crisis." Although there were many reports, the vast majority repeated the central theme that these minors are coming to the United States because of the violence in their home countries (and for the American Dream, of course). Occasionally, the theme shifted. After a few months of reporting this story, media coverage dropped off quite a bit. Then it picked up again over the period of June and July of 2015. Two themes pervade almost all the coverage. First is the standard "a year later" report. The second is that Mexico is helping to stop these minors before they arrive at the U.S. border. So the story line hangs in the balance as set by media outlets. The more significant point here revolves around the mediums of information. With the content firmly rooted in basic myth as a commodified narrative, it dissolves. Similar to the "Blacks" in Barthes "Bichon" critique, the Central American immigrant minor dissolves in a pool of North American mythology through its image. The vision remains fragmented and distant or as Barthes (1957/2012) words it, "Myth deprives the object of which it speaks of all history. In it, history evaporates" (p. 264). The content itself is myth; the mediums of mythology seal the box of context and all the reporting collapses inward.

Harvest of Empire or Syncretism

Basically, the immigrant crisis would be better served unreported because when the spectacle of the immigrant minor threatens to appear in full view, it becomes a mirror (Barthes, 2012, p. 256). This mirror functions paradoxically. It reflects the image of the viewer *and* of the Other. The viewer is generally in the position to define the Other in accordance to the viewer or to perceive the viewer in the Other or to wish to see sameness in the Other. So the mirror operates as a lens to look at and through. This lens sharpens the image the more the sameness is achieved. With the correct lens, the "Blacks" juxtaposed with Bichon can generate some civilized whiteness. A more fitting example is Barthes (1957/2012) discussion of the *Lost Continent*, a 1954 Italian film that exoticizes Southeast Asia. He notes:

> The East is ready for the disappearing act our film has in readiness for it … our studio ethnologists will have no difficulty postulating an East formally exotic, [but] in reality deeply resembling the West. Orientals have religions of their own? No problem, the differences are insignificant compared to the deep unity of idealism. (p. 185)

As the Other comes into focus in the mirror, it more closely resembles the viewer. The constructed nature of media images plays a role, but within all mediums, construction is assumed. Thus, going beyond the construction of myth, the medium fulfills its totalizing function of reflection. Inserting (injecting) Central American immigrant minors into the medium automatically results in the viewer's attempt at sameness. When the viewer sees less of the Other, the Other is no longer the Other (disappears). Barthes uses the word syncretism to describe this technique of assimilation.

The documentary film *Harvest of Empire* (2012) serves as a fitting contemporary example of syncretism. Principally the structure of the film is very basic. It employs the same technical and organizational structure as most documentaries with slick production, emotionally driven (ethnic) music, and a slight sense of urgency. The narrative focuses on U.S. intervention in the affairs of several Latin American countries and the subsequent immigration of people to the United States. Without much effort, one can find a wealth of information detailing the *atrocities* of U.S. intervention in Latin America and particularly Central America. One source where this information is only briefly approached is the film *Harvest of Empire*. This film represents the progressive liberal take on the immigration debate and is supposed to provide some historical context. In reality, the film operates as medium of disappearance of the Latino by its absorption into acceptable North American cultural practices.

One striking example concerns Mexican immigration into the United States. The image of crosses (fatalities) on the border wall separating Mexico and the United States provides the potential for appearance. The viewer flinches with discomfort upon first sight. The first mirror image delivers a more focused approach to the issues.

Enrique Morones, founder of Border Angels alludes to the "deep unity" or "deep resemblance" of the neighboring people. With earnest sincerity he passionately pleas to the viewer, "We know that the American people, like the Mexican people, and the people all over the world are good people and they want to do the right thing. But they need to know what's happening in order to do the right thing." His basic thesis (and the thesis of the film, as well) is that if people are informed, they will act according to the information provided. So there exists a common human spirit of goodness that transcends national, ethnic, racial, and cultural differences. More importantly, that this human goodness disposed of ignorance sets aside all the political and historical context of relations. Visually and aurally Morones represents the focusing of the lens to reflect sameness in the eyes of the viewer. He is disappearing (as Mexican) before our eyes as the memory of the ten thousand border deaths, mentioned just seconds before Morones declares Americans inherently good but ignorant, dissolves.

Is it really a case of Americans being uninformed? Or is it possible that the mediums in which Americans are informed precludes action through the absorption and dissolving of the information? To further illustrate the point, the viewer is introduced to Dr. Alfredo Quiñones-Hinojosa, the director of the Brain Tumor Program at John Hopkins. His character serves the role of official disappearance. He *is* sameness. Dr. Quiñones-Hinojosa retells the American Dream narrative of hard work and reward in the United States, which implies the separation of the immigrant labor class. After a short and decontextualized comment on NAFTA, Dr. Quiñones-Hinojosa's voiceover is coupled with a photo of him wearing an American Major League Baseball cap. In this instance his image is a mirror. He fulfills the viewer's narcissistic urge as a subjective reflection. Whereas Morones' image retains a shred of authentic Mexican, Quiñones-Hinojosa mirrors the viewer's reflection.

Dr. Quiñones-Hinojosa returns to the screen to cement his depoliticized sameness with the viewer. While sitting in his office in a medical doctor uniform (costume) he states:

> My whole objective is to try to pay back. How do I do that? By practicing science and trying to be the best brain surgeon I can possibly be so that one day I can find a better way to treat brain cancer. We are all humans. We all have the same abilities. We all have the same potential. The question is: How do you take advantage of that potential?

In the context of the brief review of Mexican tragedies relayed in the film, the viewer may be deceived to think that the answer to his question of "paying back" would include somehow paying back Mexican immigrants directly in some kind of way. Perhaps he could have discussed his activism as one who supports radical open immigration. But those responses would have defied Barthes claims on myth. Seen through the clearer lens of progressive sameness, this character must relieve the viewer of the potential appearance by repeating Morones' previous assertion of human oneness. Also, his peculiar pronoun change from "we" to "you" aptly transmits the message of separation and disappearance. He never answers his final question concerning individual potential. That is for them (Mexican immigrants) to answer.

The tautological underpinnings of human connectedness that Morones and Quiñones-Hinojosa (and the entire film) assert relates to the godlike cloud that hovers over the entire landscape (metaphorically). This assertion augments the mythos of the American Dream. With tenuous evidence, the entire production of the image (issue) of immigration recirculates to the beginning of the Western Hemisphere's history and to the ideology of Manifest Destiny. In this case, the image colonizes the weaker (unsuspecting) image. The image of the doctor colonizes the image of the farm worker. The image of comfort colonizes the image of poverty. The image of happiness colonizes the image of desolation. When the more powerful image colonizes the weaker image in media, the powerful image negates the weaker. The weaker image is forgotten and disappears in the context. In *Harvest of Empire*, the chronological succession (precession) of worst to best images in the brief examination of each Latin American country exemplifies the only acceptable rhetorical strategy. But rhetoric itself is no longer a conscious strategy. It has also been colonized to the point of unrecognizability. The medium swallows rhetoric because the medium is rhetoric. The film's procession of exploited immigrants to liberal hopes to documented success stories illustrates a social Darwinist precession that revolves around the tautology of universal sameness and North American liberty.

In contrast, as an exploitative documentary, *The Lost Continent* reveals disappearance. The viewer is placed into a position to consume a faraway culture that is constructed in such a way as to become Western. Barthes (1957/2012) offers two possible alternatives for the image of the Other. He writes, "Either to acknowledge the Other as another Punch and Judy show or to render it harmless as a pure reflection of the West" (p. 186). *The Lost Continent* achieves both alternatives in its explicit exploitative qualities. Perhaps to a 1954 viewer, the film appeared to be an authentic portrayal of the Orient. With contemporary eyes, the film appears as both the Punch and Judy show and a harmless exoticized reflection. But *Harvest of Empire* is meant to be taken as a serious documentary. Surely the filmmakers did not intend to create a harmless reflection of Latino immigrants as North Americans. With intent aside, the film fulfills its function to temper movement and solidify sameness. The documentary film medium cannot do otherwise. The inclusion of immigrant images on film marks the commencement of the immigrant as a concrete subject. To recall Boorstin, the entire film is a "pseudo-event." Any spontaneous appearance of the immigrant folds inward through the image.

So the visual mediums, such as film or digital video, necessitate disappearance. Barthes (1957/2012) mentions the placement of foreign refugees on film. He notes, "It is the same for refugees, a long procession of whom is shown at the start of the film making their way down a mountain; futile, of course, to locate them: they are eternal essences of refugees, it is in the nature of the East to produce them" (p. 186). Countless media images of Latino immigrants fill visual outlets. *Harvest of Empire* is only one small example that reinforces the idea of the production of refugees from

Latin America. Does the viewer of the image see anything other than production? In a sense, that is who they are and what they do. They immigrate. They move to North America.

Figure 1. Leaked photo of a U.S. Border Patrol's processing center.
Breitbart News Network

The appropriation of this particular image stands as a testament to the fragile nature of image production and consumption. Putting aside social or political considerations of the image, it merely exists as fractured entity to be absorbed and/ or digested by the viewer (perceiver). The obvious (and logical) conclusion is the disposal of the image as a waste product. This occurs because the image cannot reflect the power subject. Therefore it dissolves. To locate the moment the image dissolves is problematized by the medium. This image comes after concrete engagement. The photographer holds the image and shares the image. It emits from a screen or even as a concrete paper product. The image lives on a computer screen in the vastness of same images. This is why all considerations that relate to meaning within information production (political, economic, cultural, etc.) hold zero value. The viewer perceives an image like this, and then sees another, followed by another, to infinity. Each image configures cancelation. A reversibility where intent contradicts then implodes. The journalist or the agent presents the photo with a purpose (good or bad/positive or negative). This purpose drowns in the reversibility of image proliferation.

For example, if the image of the immigrant minors in the processing center is to elicit discourse or public outcry, the medium of the image determines how

41

discourse develops. In this case, the overwhelming number of images reverses the intent and cancels discourse (or outcry). The medium includes the outcry. As Barthes (1957/2012) asserts concerning the image of the Guatemalan Communists, "someone shuddered for us, reflected for us, [and] judged for us" (p. 116). Although appropriated, the image is not open for interpretation. It sticks (transfixed) inside an immense network of prejudice, bias, and previously fashioned beliefs. The viewer absorbs. It is the only plausible option within the confines of the image medium (computer screen, smart phone screen, television screen, theater screen).

THE IMAGE

The revolution will not be televised. (Gil Scott-Heron)

The revolution *will* be televised and thus a revolution *will not* actually take place. The question is: how do we keep the revolution from being televised? A more apt question for the contemporary moment is: how do we keep the revolution from being digitalized (imagized)? Once placed into digitalization, the revolution will not be a revolution, but a pseudo-event. It will be nothing more than an image of constructed artificial revolution. In terms of Central American immigrant minors, the digital pseudo-event negates the spontaneous event. Like *The Lost Continent* or *Harvest of Empire*, action melts away on the screens of computers and smart phones into buttons and clicks. To paraphrase Baudrillard, the event dies and "images are not the sites of the 'production of meaning' but rather, 'sites of the disappearance of meaning and representation'" (Coulter, 2004, p. 1).

An appropriate illustration of this model concerns the reinsertion of the real into the mediums of the image. To provide a specific example, an educational professional employed by a large school district in the southeastern United States held a formal presentation that discussed the immigrant population in the classroom. The educator used a visual medium with many images of the students. The content of the presentation revolved around the lack of success at every level in educating these students. But the central thesis focused on the immigrant students taking ownership over their own learning. Apart from the gross decontextualization of the difficult circumstances of the student population (many, if not most, faced desperate trials to traverse the desert to get to the border [which may explain their lack of achievement, among other reasons]), the presentation turned the students into images. By doing this, the students no longer held a space in concrete reality. Similar to the treatment of the "red negroes of Africa" in *Paris-Match*, the students became a "puppet show" and "a pure object ... a clown" (Barthes, 2012, pp. 68, 266). The educator added comments about physical appearance to further objectify the students. Certainly, it was not the educator's intent to turn the students into a spectacle, but something compels the dehumanization of the Other.

To further explain, the Central American immigrant minor enters the classroom as an image. The teacher sees the image of the real before seeing the real. The real complicates the image. Therefore, the image must regain the status of privilege or the preferred mode of engagement from subject to object. The image does not speak. If the image speaks within a medium of media, the speech is filtered, manipulated, whitewashed and so forth. Even in the case where the image speaks in patterns of distress (or in realty), the medium destructs the message or overcomes the message. The discomfort of the image's potential to speak as a human subject (appearance), causes a disruption of the narcissistic drive. In order to avoid this discomfort, the teacher must employ various mechanisms similar to those stated earlier by Barthes. To summarize: either transform the object into a kind of minstrel show or into a harmless subjective reflection.

Another way to examine the deflection of this moment of appearance is to build a replica of the real. By relegating the Other to the status of image, a double enters immaterial existence. This double threatens to "contaminate reality" (Baudrillard, 1987, p. 16). The contamination of reality is like the contamination of a pristine water source. The contamination may occur slowly and may be unnoticeable. Eventually the entire water source is contaminated, but all reference to a pristine water source becomes and then remains elusive. Hence, the contaminated water is the only water and because of this fact, it is no longer contaminated. In this sense, the image of the immigrant minor replaces the real immigrant minor. The image becomes the real through the visual medium. Educators and the like see only the acutely propagated appropriations and any reference to the real immigrant minor is unlocatable. The specific attempt to relocate the vision of the minor in the vision of the aforementioned presentation represents the subtle though obscene relegation of the Other to a fixed vision of concrete objectivity. The image cannot move. Its disposal is imminent and fortifies the narcissistic model of productivity. Baudrillard (1987) reaffirms: "[the image] appropriates reality for its own ends ... [and] it anticipates the point that the real no longer has time to be produced as such" (p. 16). The educator proved incapable of reproducing the real in the image. Instead the image produced the real (because the image overwhelms the real).

Again, the content of the educator's presentation revolved around the lack of success at every level in educating the immigrant minors. The lack of success held its basis in the non-reflecting mirror. The more the students displayed resistance to objectivity, the more they failed to achieve. Essentially, their failure orbited around a displaced center (the core of subjectivity). Within the center lays the sameness of reflection. In order to subdue the object, the image must be docile, happy, engaged and smiling. The images contradicted the verbal and written word. Happy teenagers who fail to succeed. It appears obvious that the image mitigates the failure. The educator defined this ambiguity subtextually through an interface of a dispersion of liability. The concept of taking ownership speaks from the rhetoric of capital (excellence) and is illogical and impossible. Immigrant minors cannot take ownership of the classroom while simultaneously the educator cannot freely take ownership of the students without mitigating their appearance. The students funnel through a metaphorically cosmological filtering of object reproduction. If the reproduction is not met (successful mirroring of the subject), they are smiling failures.

The true crux of this obscene presentation rests in the idea that the real student reflects the failure of the educator, but this reflection is the wrong reflection. Baudrillard (1970/1998) claims, "narcissism [is] laid down in advance by models produced industrially by the mass media … Everyone finds his or her own personality in living up to these models" (p. 96). The image of the smiling students is the narcissistic urge that is supplanted by the contradictory report of failure. If the immigrant students succeed and retain subjectivity, they fail to fulfill the mass media model. If the immigrant students fail and retain subjectivity, they also fail to fulfill the mass media model. The intervention occurs when the educator, whether consciously aware of the model or not, generates the model. Again, to generate the model of realized narcissism, the educator must invoke the proper image (as in *Harvest of Empire*): the happy student who does not succeed. This relinquishes all responsibility and maintains the narcissistic reflection.

The object takes primacy over the subject in this reversibility of power. The object (the image of the immigrant minor) remains secondary in manifested concrete power, but overcomes the subject by losing its own concrete reality. So its objectivity as an image replaces the appearance of the real. In this reversibility the subject needs the object to perceive the circular power. Without the image construction of the object the subject can never realize the moment of dismissal of the object and its own domination (North American technocrats over the immigrant minors). But the subject manifests power only over an illusory object, the image of the immigrant minor. This is what makes the image so significant in dissolving the real. This epitomizes the mediums at work. The object cannot be real or else power relations may be troubled.

To repeat Barthes (1957/2012), the image driven "myth deprives the object of which it speaks of all history. In it, history evaporates" (p. 264). The history of the border crossing and possibly of previous academic success dissolves. Its replacement is the requisite gratefulness illustrated through the smile, and the traditional high rate of failure in school. The image must align with the model. The border crossing pictures an imaginary flight repeated for months in mediums which facilitate and inherently liquefy the spontaneous event. Once the border crossers manifest the proper North American image, it is too late to recapture the real. This is the case in good or bad terms. Both proliferate on the screen.

The cultural transformation required to overcome this inevitable dilemma evaporates with consumption. One who consumes the image (through purchase of prerequisite commodities) also (re)produces the image. So production and consumption occur simultaneously. The image is already in place. The image of Narcissus is already in the water before he looks. The educator only knows the image model (the global narcissistic urge of capital [the world through the eyes of North America] leaves the educator without a choice and without the knowledge of a choice) and places it before the students. The students consume (clothing, speech, food, etc.) and reproduce the predetermined image. Although Native Maya make up a large number of the students, the educator's images exclusively reproduced the predetermined model rendering the Maya invisible.

THE POSSIBILITY OF AN ENCOUNTER AND THE DISCURSIVE PRACTICE OF DÉTOURNEMENT

What happens in East Pakistan or for that matter Birmingham, any historic event, anywhere is always on the far side of the frontier of the publicity dream. What happens 'out there,' happens to strangers, whose fate is meant to be different to ours, what happens in the dream is meant to happen to us. (John Berger)

Berger's profound statement requires the question: What happens when the far away stranger enters the dream of the viewer? Berger (1972) points to the functions of images in media. Images of violence, poverty and so on, happen in places far away (possibly called nightmares), while images of glamour, security and success encompass the dream of the viewer. Basically, the Central American immigrant minor's nightmare invades the dream of the North American technician (an educator, for example). Until the literal/physical point of entrance into the physical space of the North American, the encounter is mediated by the disposable images of the faraway nightmare (the border holding center, for instance), a fate not meant for the technician. Since the image of the Other lacks the true representative qualities of another human being, it is *only* in the moment of the face-to-face human encounter (interaction) where a shared discourse can potentially arise; in other words: in the appearance of the subject.

To further explain the significance of this encounter, Judith Butler (2004) states "The face of the Other comes to me from outside, and interrupts that narcissistic circuit. The face of the Other calls me out of narcissism towards something finally more important" (p. 138). When one is called out of narcissism, the mirror image is disturbed, and it is also replaced. This frightens the subject. Furthermore, Slavoj Žižek (2012) explains, "the other's face makes an unconditional demand on us; we did not ask for it, and we are not allowed to refuse it" (p. 827). The visual image medium screens do not interrupt the narcissistic circuit nor make demands. The mediums' carry an all-inclusive functionality whereas the face in objective reality carries possibility. Emmanuel Levinas describes this encounter of possibility. He claims, "To be in relation with the other face to face … is the situation of discourse" (Butler, 2004, p. 138). Thus, discourse develops from the face to face encounter with the Other and, subsequently, this creates the moment of possibility. The notion of a smooth and effortless discourse within the disproportionate power dynamics of the North American technician and the immigrant minor appears challenging. As Butler and Žižek note, the face to face encounter arises without request. The immigrant student enters the space without invitation. The nightmare enters the dream. Nonetheless an ethical imperative results. The true challenge of this ethical imperative to break the narcissistic circuit rests in the dismissal of the image.

Žižek (2012) explores this idea further. He relates that "in my being taken hostage by the Other, I assume supremacy over the Other. Do we not encounter this wounded-precarious Other almost daily, in advertisements for charity which bombard us with images of starving or disfigured children crying in agony?" (p. 828). To be held hostage to the Other means that the ethical requirement, in the face to face moment, explodes within and provokes superiority. Unlike the visual images of advertisements, which are easily disposed, the concrete encounter truly unsettles. For instance, in the classroom, the teacher assumes supremacy specifically because of the frustration of feeling held hostage. The very universal human goodness propagated in *Harvest of Empire* is at the heart of the teacher's moral conflict. The helpless Other must believe in human goodness. The teacher is given the role of exemplar of human goodness. But this role is impossible to play because the premise of universal human goodness negates the firsthand experience of the immigrant minors (and the teacher). The teacher, who still remains in the position of authority, must blame the students for their lack of faith in the tautology of human goodness. At this moment, the image now has a place to manifest and replaces the real. Žižek (2012) inverts the principle of the universal and relates that those "who are 'out of place' ... stand for the universal dimension" (p. 831). The dismissal of the image is also the dismissal of the supremacy attached to the subjugation of the imagined. The ethical imperative involves the conscious recognition that the Other is the universal and that the North American technician is the exception, not only in the Western Hemisphere, but also in North America amidst the vast Other.

And so it must be asked: what constructive possibilities can grow from the encounter? With the image terminated, the face to face encounter begins the mutual discursive practice embedded in the authentic confrontation of human subjects. The face to face encounter requires a discourse that identifies the image in-itself. Simply stated the image in-itself exists and only exists. It exists without essence. To imagine the image in-itself, it must be demystified. The discourse must lift the veils of ideology. Therefore, the newly arrived immigrant minor shares (and leads) in the demystification process of seeing the image in-itself. One discursive starting point is the analysis of the current images of the immigrant minor or immigrants, in general. Generally the population group is split into three visual images: impoverished laborers, violent criminals, or American Dream success stories. These images broadcasted on countless self-effacing medium screens conflate in the reporting of pseudo-events, and because of this fact, the teacher must ask: do these three images represent the entire scope of immigrant people (especially the unaccompanied minors)?

One discursive practice teachers can utilize is "détournement", which literally means "diversion" (Vinson & Ross, 2003, p. 251) and originates as a mode of resistance promoted by the aforementioned Guy Debord and the Situationist

International. According to Anselm Jappe, "détournement involves 'a quotation, or more generally a re-use, that 'adapts' the original element to a new context' such that a given image either 1) 'may be reemployed in such a way as to modify [its] meaning'; or 2) such that 'effect may be to reinforce the real meaning of an element … by changing its form'" (as cited in Vinson & Ross, 2003, pp. 252–253).

Figure 2. Photo altered of a young happy child going to school.
www.inquisitr.com, 7 April 2015

This image illustrates the discursive practice of détournement. Obviously, the image could be altered much more elaborately to relay the "real" meaning and must be accompanied by a discussion. Nonetheless, the context of the image is adapted. Teachers and students can introduce a wide range of media images (some with text) for countless adaptations. The variety of perspectives advances the conversation and facilitates the release of multiple ideas. Détournement demystifies the photos by challenging the image mythos frequently dispersed. The above image (the American Dream motif) when altered casts a new or real meaning to the audience and also conveys a message from the one who adapts the image. This method requires teachers to see the encounter as an opportunity for mutual engagement in order to overcome the negation of the student by the image. Of course, this transcends all moments of encounter with Central American immigrant minors and thus the possibility to revive the appearance of the real.

REFERENCES

Achbar, M., & Wintonick, P. (1992). *Manufacturing consent: Noam Chomsky and the media* [Documentary]. United States: Necessary Illusions Productions.
Barthes, R. (2012 version). *Mythologies*. New York, NY: Hill and Wang. (Originally published in 1957)
Baudrillard, J. (1987). *The evil demon of images* (P. Patton & P. Foss, Eds.). N.S.W., Australia: Power Institute of Fine Arts, University of Sydney.
Baudrillard, J. (1994). *Simulacra and simulation*. Ann Arbor, MI: University of Michigan. (Originally published in 1981)
Baudrillard, J. (1996). *The perfect crime*. London: Verso.

Baudrillard, J. (1998). *The consumer society: Myths and structures.* London: Sage. (Originally published in 1970)

Berger, J. (1972). *John Berger / Ways of seeing, Episode 4* [Video]. Retrieved from https://www.youtube.com/watch?v=5jTUebm73IY

Boorstin, D. J. (1992). *The image: A guide to pseudo-events in America.* New York, NY: Vintage. (Original work published in 1962)

Butler, J. (2004). *Precarious life: The powers of mourning and violence.* London: Verso.

Coulter, G. (2004). Reversibility: Baudrillard's 'One great thought.' *International Journal of Baudrillard Studies, 1*(2), 1–1. Retrieved on June 21, 2015.

Debord, G. (1990). *Comments on the society of the spectacle.* London: Verso.

Debord, G. (1994). *The society of the spectacle.* New York, NY: Zone. (Originally published in 1967)

Getzels, P., & Lopez, E. (2012). *Harvest of empire* [Documentary]. United States: Onyz Films.

Gras, E., Moser, G., & Bonzi, L. (1955). *Lost continent* [Documentary]. Italy: Astra Cinematografica.

McLuhan, M. (1967). *Marshal McLuhan interview 1967.* July 2009. Retrieved July 7, 2015, from https://www.youtube.com/watch?v=OMEC_HqWlBY

North, J. (2014, July 9). How the US's foreign policy created an immigrant refugee crisis on its own southern border. *The Nation.* Retrieved from http://www.thenation.com/article/how-uss-foreign-policy-created-immigrant-refugee-crisis-its-own-southern-border/

Project Censored. (2015, July 8). *The news that didn't make the news and why* [Website]. Retrieved from www.projectcensored.org

Rich, B. (2008). *To uphold the world: The message of Ashoka and Kautilya for the 21st century.* New Delhi: Viking.

Scott-Heron, G. (1970). The revolution will not be televised. On *Small Talk at 125th and Lenox* [CD]. RCA.

Vinson, K. D., & Ross, E. W. (2003). Controlling images, the power of high-stakes testing. In K. Saltman & D. Gabbard (Eds.), *Education as enforcement, the militarization and corporatization of schools* (pp. 241–257). New York, NY: Routledge.

Žižek, S. (2012). *Less than nothing: Hegel and the shadow of dialectical materialism.* London: Verso.

JONATHAN RYAN

5. MOBILIZING A COMMUNITY

We must look in the mirror as a nation and remember who we are and who we want to be. As I say to people: Do you know why it's so expensive to be the beacon of hope and liberty in the world? Because it is very much worth it!

(Ryan, J. 2014 before Congress)

Live Speech delivered by Jonathan Ryan at the LIRS (Lutheran Immigrant and Refugee Services) Convening in Tuscon, AZ on September 3, 2014:

I would like to begin by thanking LIRS for bringing us all together during this unique time to consider how we will respond to what is now the challenge of our time. The Refugee and Immigrants Center for Education and Legal Services, or RAICES, has been serving vulnerable populations of refugees and victims of torture since 1986. It is during these times of perceived crisis that we experience firsthand what our community and our country are all about. We also get to see what it means for those people around the world who long for the freedom and liberty that we so routinely take for granted. I am honored to be given this time to share with you what we have learned in Texas over the past few months.

Our mission at RAICES is to protect refugees. In furtherance of this mission, we assist unaccompanied children to navigate the complicated immigration court system and to better understand their rights and responsibilities within that process. Starting on June 9th of this past summer (2014), we began providing know your rights presentations and individual legal screenings to the nearly 1,200 children that were detained at the Lackland Air Force Base in San Antonio, Texas.

We completed more than 2,000 intakes with these children, and after careful and thorough peer review we determined that more than 63 percent have strong claims for asylum or other forms of humanitarian protection under our current immigration laws.

RAICES' has many years of experience and we have more than a 98 percent success rate in cases we assigned to *pro bono* representatives using this selection criteria. Thus, our legal findings are supported by literally hundreds of positive adjudications on behalf of our unaccompanied minor clients.

The children we served at Lackland and in the more than 1,100 other shelter beds in San Antonio and Corpus Christi are fleeing unspeakable violence. The

M. López-Stafford Levy (Ed.), Children from the Other America, 49–53.

vast majority of them are from the northern triangle countries of El Salvador, Honduras and Guatemala. Our interviews have confirmed that a majority of them are victims of sexual assault, trafficking, gang intimidation, persecution and even government-sponsored torture.

Our staff and our volunteers have met with girls as young as 12 years old who have fled their countries to escape sexual exploitation. The phenomenon that is occurring in these countries can literally be described as a war against children in which young boys as old as 8 or 9 are given food toys and money to transport drugs and as they get older it turns into intimidation and death threats against them and their families, used to force them to join these organizations in what is now a new, normalized criminal violence that is rampant and widespread across these countries, and also in Mexico.

These children and their families who have faced such violence and difficult conditions have made a conscious decision to undertake a life-threatening and dangerous journey because they understand that to stay is to die. A woman in Honduras was recently interviewed about why she had allowed her daughter to travel alone from Honduras to the United States. In her response, this mother stated, "I would rather find out that my daughter died trying to get to freedom than to see her shot dead on my front doorstep."

Just as the number of unaccompanied children crossing the border has ticked down, we have been faced with a new challenge, one that we thought had been defeated years ago: family detention.

I am holding in my hands today a document that I received from the Department of Homeland Security last week. Our government is now filing this evidence packet right here in every single case where the attorney or family request an immigration judge set an immigration bond so that a mother and her children can be released from detention.

On these pages, senior members of our Department of Homeland Security sign declarations stating that the presence of women and children on our border is a threat to our national security.

This is a crisis, and this is a threat to our national security. The threat to our national security is that the most powerful country in history of this world, the country that liberated itself from colonial domination, the country that freed Europe from the Nazis, that held back the Soviet Union, that was attacked and said, "Let's roll," is now declaring that women and children seeking our protection are a threat to our national security.

This is a crisis of confidence that begs us dust to dust off a proud, old American saying, one that has been evoked in times of real existential threats to our way of life: the only thing we have to fear, is fear itself.

How we respond to this current humanitarian need, in which families and children are fleeing in every direction in search of protection, speaks to the moral character of our nation. The decisions we make now have the potential to bolster our human rights record or, in fact, undermine our ability to hold other actors and nations accountable for their human rights records.

I am so proud of my staff and volunteers for their tireless and often thankless efforts over the course of this summer. We know first-hand that by affording these children proper screening for trafficking and persecution, as well as the opportunity to be represented by counsel and receive fair and full consideration of their asylum applications could well mean the difference between life and death.

At RAICES we were faced with a choice, early this summer, when the government opened its Emergency Reception Center at Lackland Air Force Base. We knew that we had the knowledge, experience and ability to provide the civil legal aid response was so desperately needed there. However, our government was very clear no federal funding would be provided to support our services at the base.

I was reminded in our comparatively small predicament of my friend, and former client, Kevin Merida. Kevin is from Guatemala and left his home five years ago. When Kevin learned his life was in immediate danger, he left his home with no money, no plan and without even telling his mother goodbye.

Kevin joined up with companions along his journey. Together, they shared what little they had or could find and they looked out for each other. They even rode on top of a freight train called "The Beast," because of the limbs that it has mangled and the lives that it has taken. He was robbed; he had to pay bribes to members of the police to avoid deportation; and he was constantly in jeopardy of falling into the hands of traffickers and organized criminal syndicates such as the Zetas.

Kevin left his home because he knew that staying put was not an option. Kevin found safety by joining others with whom he shared a common experience and common goals, because he knew he could not make it alone. Kevin jumped onto The Beast because he knew that without taking a risk, he could not move forward.

Today, Kevin is a US Legal Permanent Resident, graduated from high school with honors in English and speaks in public with fellow former unaccompanied children about his own experience. And, I am proud to say, in October of this year, Kevin will become a proud member of the US Marine Corps.

Kevin accomplished all of this because he was able to access a *pro bono* civil legal aid attorney at RAICES who helped him to prepare his immigration case. As Kevin himself says, he could not have won his case alone and, had he been sent back to Guatemala, today he would probably be dead.

But just like the group he traveled with cross Mexico, we, like Kevin, know inaction is not an option. Like the generation of men and women who fought in World War II – a generation we now know as "The Greatest Generation," who saw and who understood the genocide and mass murder of people just because of who they are is a harm to all of humanity that can never be tolerated. We know through our work with asylum seekers, refugees and others who have suffered extreme violence and abuse, once lost, the lighthouse of freedom and democracy may never again be lit. So, we work hard to keep its light shining for us, for our children and for the entire world.

We gather together here from different parts of the world and represent many different disciplines. But we all share fundamental beliefs, principles and goals: the sanctity of life, the dignity of the individual and the right of all people to self-determination and security in their persons. These ideals unite us, they inspire us and they remind us the daily chores of our work tap into the very marrow of this nation's greatest legacy, as enshrined in our Declaration of Independence, our Constitution and the refugee and asylum laws I so proudly practice. To accomplish our goal, we too, need one another.

Something we learned this summer when analyzing our own data is indigenous, Guatemalan girls – though individually some of the most vulnerable people – in fact had experienced safer journeys compared with their Honduran El Salvadoran counterparts. We believe this is due to the linguistic, social and cultural bonds shared by these indigenous children who travel together in intact groups from beginning all the way to the end.

Finally, and without a doubt most importantly, we must not allow fear to guide our actions, and we must be willing to take risks. As you engage in this topic, I want to challenge each of you to hold on to this image: a young girl, running alongside of The Beast, reaching out, trying to grasp on. Will she slip? Will she hold on? Will someone lend her hand and pull her up? She doesn't know, but still she runs until she reaches her goal, because she has no other option than to move forward on her path.

We, as advocates, are just like this girl. We are all here with one foot on the ground and a hand on The Beast. We know we cannot go backwards. We know we must rely on one another to get through this. We know we must have at least as much courage and be as willing to take risks like the clients we serve have all done.

This summer, my agency, RAICES, faced a very uncertain future. There were days when I thought we were on the verge of closing, or simply at the point of falling apart. But we stuck together, we held on and we made it. This far.

Today, I stand before you from on top of The Beast, and I am seeking your help to continue my journey. I am here, extending my hand and inviting you to also take a leap of faith and to join us. Together, we will all find America. Thank you.

Figure 1. Courtesy of RAICES-San Antonio, Texas 2014

PETER ROOS AND MICHELE LÓPEZ-STAFFORD LEVY

6. AN INTERVIEW WITH PETER ROOS

For the U.S. education system, there were a series of laws passed regarding equitable access for children in schools and public education in general. Brown v. Board of Education occurred in 1954. Ten years later was the Civil Rights Act of 1964 followed by the Bilingual Education Act of 1968 and the Equal Opportunity Act of 1974 and yet these laws were not being adhered to for the children in the state of Florida. A grass roots effort took place with strong support to bring a lawsuit and ultimately culminated in the passage of the Florida Consent Decree. *Approved in 1990, the decree assured attention and responsiveness for non-English speakers.*

Peter Roos, civil rights attorney for Multicultural Education, Training and Advocacy (META), granted the authors an interview in celebration of the Twenty-fifth Anniversary of the Florida Consent Decree. As phone interviews go, they capture a dialogue between people versus creating prose for reading yet the dialogue was so rich and spontaneous we made the artistic decision to keep it in this exciting format.

MSL: Can you please give us some context that led to the passage of the Florida Consent Decree of 1990, Peter?

PR: Sure. The 1964 Civil Rights Act which was specifically designed to end segregation in primarily the south (U.S.) included a prohibition against national origin discrimination. In the late 1960's, there was also the passage of the first federal Bilingual Education Act. The law was Title VII which wasn't a mandate but was a law that school districts could apply for funds to assist and work with Limited English Proficient (LEP and an outdated term) students.

During the early 1970's, we started picking up in terms of litigation and in terms of legislation around the country (U.S.). There was in California for example, a viable Education bill passed in 1974 called the Chacon Mosconi Act, which mandated bilingual education not just affirmative action on behalf of English Language Learners and it mandated native language instruction under certain circumstances if you had sufficient numbers of kids, at grade level, etc.

There began to be litigation enforcing the Civil Rights Act and I believe in 1974 a case that relied upon it from San Francisco reached the Supreme Court, Lau v. Nichols. It ruled unanimously that there was an obligation under the 1964 Civil Rights Act to take affirmative steps to deal with the needs of the Limited English

M. López-Stafford Levy (Ed.), Children from the Other America, 55–63.

Proficient kids. Soon thereafter, Congress encapsulated the Lau ruling and so made it federal law requiring school districts and states had to intelligently respond to the needs of these children. It is known as the Equal Educational Opportunity Act of 1974, and has been used by ever since to protect the rights of English learners.

In the late 1970's and early 1980's the courts began to impose obligations on states as well as individual school districts. These cases from Texas, Idaho, California and Illinois informed our actions in Florida.

MSL: Yes.

Peter: U.S. v Texas (Bilingual-5281) and a victory in Colorado—Keyes v School District each led to a bilingual decree. There were several other major cases...

MSL: Like Plyler v Doe?

Peter: Plyler dealt with the rights of the undocumented.

MSL: Okay.

Peter: Texas passed a law to exclude undocumented kids and in 1982 the Supreme Court struck that down.

MSL: I see, sticking to language rights. I see your focus. Good, good.

Peter: It is relevant to what we're talking about in Florida as I will explain later. In the 1980's there were several other cases decided. One such case of significance was Castañeda v. Pickard in south Texas.

MSL: Yep.

Peter: In that case, the Fifth Circuit Court ruled bilingual education, per se, was not required but set up a whole rubric for analyzing whether states or schools were delivering programs responsive to LEP children. Castañeda was filed by the Legal Aid Program in Harlingen, TX.

MSL: Like MALDEFF (Mexican-American Legal Defense and Educational Fund)?

Peter: Um, no. It was actually done by TRLA, Texas Rural Legal Assistance. I was at MALDEF most of the time we're talking about and was involved in the Colorado case and a statewide language case in Texas, USA v. Texas. MALDEF and others assisted the people at TRLA. Castañeda was sort of a mixed bag. The 5th Circuit set a standard for analyzing schools or school districts, requiring, then to adopt theoretically programs to address needs, to put resources into their programs to properly implement their adopted program and to monitor student progress.

MSL: Please tell us about that.

Peter: Yes, first of all you had to have a theoretically sound program. Second, you had to put resources into the theoretically sound program and implement it, so that the kids would learn English and subject matter and not find themselves left behind. And finally there had to be a monitoring component to assure that if it wasn't working, you would change the approach. The overall goal was to try to assure that kids were learning English in such a way so that they could compete with their English speaking peers and not fall behind. While native language instruction was not required, it could be part of the solution.

So, now we're into the mid 1980's, I had moved from MALDEF to META (Multicultural Education, Training and Advocacy) and started working with Rosie (Castro-Feinberg) to look at Florida and how it measured up with the standards I just articulated. Rosie was an old friend of all of ours. We were all working nationally with NABE (National Association of Bilingual Education) and she (Rosie) was on the Dade County School Board for part of the time and she's a friend so she regularly beseeched us, if you know Rosie...

MSL: (chuckling with Peter) Right?

Peter: She basically beseeched us to come on down and sue the state of Florida. So I got involved and Camilo Perez who was also in our office, and we met with a number of organizations and individuals who were concerned with the education and what we concluded was the state of Florida was far out of compliance with the legal standards. Essentially no state law existed, no state-wide mandate for anybody to do anything, so education of LEP students in Florida was really hit or miss and it was mostly miss. Stefan Rosenzweig who had moved from California and was working with a legal service program in Key West also signed on.

MSL: (sneers)

Peter: There were a few programs in south Florida...

MSL: Sure.

Peter: There was one notable program in Coral Gables, involving more affluent children. That got international attention. The program was at Coral Way. But even in Dade County, especially if you were not wealthy and a Cuban you were unlikely to get anything that resembled legally, adequate services, so low income kids, non-English speaking kids even in Dade County and Broward County, were not getting much; and once you got outside of south Florida where there were a significant number of immigrants, really nothing was happening.

MSL: Okay, I can feel a shift to the conversation coming about the Florida Consent Decree and I want to ask you...I can feel we're shifting into second gear now, huh?

I was born in 1960 and Fidel Castro had just taken over the island. I'm an El Pasoan now living in Broward County and employed in Ft. Lauderdale and I love all the diversity down here. We're educating Haitian-Americans and Cuban-Americans among many Latinos and my question to you is, I remember so many Cubans coming to El Paso (TX) because we speak Spanish beautifully in EP, it is a way of life and it is accepted. Anglos speak Spanish and Mexican-Americans speak English and really a lot of NABE presidents come out of EP—Josie Tinajero, Elena Izquierdo out of the University of Texas at El Paso (UTEP), Ana Huerta-Macias former President of TESOL from NMSU and UTEP which is my former stomping ground and where I was adjunct faculty. Colleagues used to say that the Bilingual Education Act happened because of the Cubans.

Peter: Cubans in Florida were contributors but focused, understandably, primarily on themselves.

MSL: Oh? Thanks for the clarification. So it really was the Californians and Texans making a big noise in '64 and we did have a Texan in office—Johnson.

Peter: Well, uh, the '64 Civil Rights Act wasn't focused on English language proficient kids. The 1964 Civil Rights Act was passed because all the efforts from "Brown" forward and had not resulted in much desegregation. The theory of the '64 Civil Rights Act was if the federal government withheld money from the school districts who discriminated they could accomplish what the court had been unable to do. The courts of course were basically charged with the enforcement of the federal act. The judges were generally white and unsympathetic in the south (U.S.) so they had a lot of problems.

LEP interests were incidental. Congress was primarily thinking about desegregating southern schools. Nevertheless, the 1964 Act applied to all discrimination of national origin minorities and was useful for ELLs. In '68 however, there was this important federal provision for Bilingual Education known as Title VII.

MSL: Funding, yes! And they sent teachers to school for free.

Peter: They had teacher training.

MSL: So now let's shift gears. You said things were deplorable in Florida all through the 1980's and so now I think we are in 1990. Correct?

Peter: We put together a coalition. The lawyers decided if we were to sue, we wanted a coalition of multiple groups and the coalition that *was* put together was made up of a variety of Floridians.

So the lawsuit was brought on behalf of ASPIRA (a Puerto Rican group) Cuban groups, LULAC (League of "United" Latin American Citizens), which is primarily a Mexican group, and on behalf of the Haitian Refugee Center. The NAACP (National Association for the Advancement of Colored People) joined in also. It was the Broward County NAACP that got the state chapter involved.

There was a woman who was a very forward thinking with the BC NAACP who got the state-wide NAACP to join in because we assured her that we were concerned with an over-representation of kids in classes for the intellectually impaired and we were concerned about *non*-placement of blacks as well as English learners into Gifted and Talented (GT) programs. It's amazing how much came together. On the eve of filing the law suit, Betty Castor who was the Superintendent of Public Instruction contacted the head of one of our organizations who was quite a prominent Cuban Civil Rights leader—a guy by the name of Oswaldo Soto. He was also tied into the Democratic Party and she (Betty) said, "I understand you want to sue us, I'd like an opportunity to meet and see if we can work things out".

Peter: (cont.) We agreed to speak as long as it was understood that if we did work something out it would have to be embedded in a court order. They agreed, and we started talking. We spent maybe over a year in negotiations and the upshot of this, as you know, is the Consent Decree then approved by the Federal courts. The court granted its approval the same day the State Board of Education approved the Decree and went into effect. That sort of is a little bit of the background – history.

MSL: Ok, I like the way you have discussed all the stakeholders (the coalition). I think that's great to show future generations that we have to leverage our resources and work together for people of many colors. My next question is, "So you've got a decree, now what?"

Peter: First of all, let's take a step back. What is in the decree? We went into negotiations with an empty slate since there was no state law or other statewide mandate. The state of Florida had no statewide mandate in terms of identifying kids. There was no statewide mandate for re-classifying kids, no mandates concerning giving LEP kids' access to the curriculum teacher "standards" were voluntary. So we had to address all of those things and this goes back to your question about Plyler.

A number of issues arose during our discussion with our clients meaningful not directly related to language issues. For example, undocumented kids, even though Plyler was decided in 1982, kids were still clearly being excluded from schools in Florida. There were also serious segregation issues.

MSL: Yes.

Peter: There were exclusions of kids in the Gifted and Talented (GT) programs with overrepresentation in Special Education (SPED/ESE) classes.

MSL: Right! Still is.

Peter: Despite all of the desegregation efforts that had taken place in Florida, LEP kids were often segregated. Some of those issues we took up early on and you'll find in the Consent Decree, there are Plyler provisions in the decree dealing with the rights of kids to go to school and checking their immigration status. There were integration issues. Normally, they would not have been in a language rights decree but they were there because of the challenges in Florida.

So, in any event, we did all of that. We went from: how do you identify kids, how you exit them and what they get inside classrooms. One of the major pieces that comes out of it is we didn't feel we could compel any particular type of instruction. Thus, we wanted to make certain the state required teachers who were fully versant with LEP issues and knew how to deal with these kids? We found ourselves in a situation whereby we had one hundred thousand (100,000) kids in Florida who were English Language Learners (ELLs), whatever the number was, going to schools back then, and a few teachers who were at the universities but it would be one hundred million years before their numbers were adequate to serve the kids who were already there who had immediate entitlement to assistance. And so this led to the in-service training for every teacher who was working with the LEP kids.

MSL: Was that in the decree, Peter?

Peter: Yes. For a number of years three hundred hours were required. It was modified and reduced to about one hundred and eighty hours. We decided in light of various circumstances to reduce the number from 300 to 180 hours but also added a provision, later, and required all principals to get something like sixty (60) hours of in-service training regarding English Language Learners. The belief was you couldn't have very much of a program if you didn't have principals with an understanding of what the program should be, and some ability to provide oversight to help the programs. The 300 hours was a very controversial thing in Florida and META became known as "*M*ake *E*very *T*eacher *A*ngry".

MSL: Ha ha. Well, you know what LEP stands for, right?—"*L*earning *E*nglish in *P*ortables".

Peter: After the Decree was signed, we actually spent a lot of time in Tallahassee assuring monitoring by the state. I do remember one issue we did address was the placement of English Language Learners in segregated surroundings.

There's one instance, I think in Palm Beach County, in which Haitian kids were placed way out in left field, literally. Anyway we filed a complaint, we negotiated with Tallahassee. We threatened them a couple of times. We may have even gone to court, then negotiated, then pulled back.

MSL: So if there's something you could tell Florida legislators about this journey and this whole process, I assume you are in California and no longer practicing law in Florida. So,

Peter: Yes, that's correct.

MSL: So if you could tell Florida legislators or the citizens of the state of Florida, you know, we're still red neck Florida and language is certainly an issue even in south Florida. I was just curious, working as hard as you did on the decree and having it in place for twenty-five years (25), it obviously has some staying power. Is there something you'd like to tell voters and lawmakers, what would you tell them Peter?

Peter: You need to have significant support for addressing the needs of ELLs in Tallahassee (your state capital's lawmakers, politicians and bureaucrats) and that began to decline when I left maybe six or seven years ago and a few years afterwards, the Florida DOE lost interest in oversight of the statewide decree. There absolutely has to be oversight of these things.

Even when you have well-meaning people, the problems, antagonisms and the like can overwhelm a good program. So, if you really want to see it succeed, there has got to be monitoring.

We/you also need to be passing legislation that provides financial assistance, 'carrots as well as sticks' to school districts to carry out good programs in a non-discriminatory way by building outside monitoring and efforts funded by foundations would also be valuable.

MSL: If you could comment on a real situation. I'm a professor in a teacher education program and I teach teachers to work with children who are non-native English speakers, right? So I send my little ducks into the world and they are out in the public schools and I get a phone call on my cell phone from one of my students who says, "We have a kid who has just arrived from Cuba, doesn't speak a lick of English and the cooperating teacher doesn't know what to do. So I said call the school district's Office of Multicultural Education and see if they can't get somebody out there; maybe as a teacher's aide, to sit in the class with the kid.

So, people really are at a loss, even teachers in the public schools on how to report? Do we call the Office of Civil Rights (OCR) when we see two, new immigrant kids in the Special Education/ESE classroom? What recourse do teachers have? This book will be for teachers.

Peter: Well, yeah. Sure. Teachers can file complaints with the OCR of the U.S. Office Department of Education. It doesn't require a lawyer. I don't know where the Florida DOE is but it ought to be concerned with these things, too. It could do that. If I were to advise a teacher, I might suggest to the teacher, the first thing she do is to try to establish a relationship with community groups to get THEM to file a complaint because retaliation is not an unknown factor and again though it is illegal (retaliation against teachers), it is a reality.

MSL: Yes, a reality.

Peter: Something that is very counterproductive.

MSL: Right.

Peter: School districts are notorious for hostility against teachers who are active in supporting migrant's rights. It is always valuable to have outsiders be the lead. Teachers can feed them the information.

MSL: Do you have any special stories like the Freedom Riders when they were on the buses in the Deep South (U.S.)? Is there any story, any reflection that you would love to share about the crazy things that goes on? You know one of my best friends is a retired Supreme Court Senior Litigator and he tells the funniest stories and I was just curious, the struggle for language rights in the state of Florida—a funny anecdote you would like to share?

Peter: There's one and it certainly comes with a lesson. When we first met with the Florida Department of Education, state the Attorney General and whatnot, we (chuckles), we felt the first meeting in Tallahassee (it was myself, Camilo Perez Stefan Rosenzweig and Rosie) all of us thought we were going to shake hands with the Attorney General and maybe Betty Castor and lay the groundwork. We ended up meeting in a conference room in the state house which was like a typical law school classroom amphitheater filled with about one hundred and fifty (150) bureaucrats.

MSL: Oh no.

Peter: The four of us were down at the bottom of the amphitheater. The first thing we were asked was, "What do you have to complain about?" And we told them. We would look at our audience as we spoke, there was always some guy in the back who would snort. And finally when we could see who this noodle was, it was a guy right out of a Burt Reynolds Smokey and the Bandit movie—your typical southern sheriff.

So after the meeting we were discussing who would be the negotiators and who was going to be doing this and that. It turns out the sheriff looking character is going to be chief negotiator for the state. So now we're totally in big trouble.

MSL: (laughter)

Peter: We thought, let's just dump these talks and get it over with! The guy's name was Lee Roberts. Turned out to be the nicest guy in the world—he just happened to have the sniffles from spring fever.

MSL: (laughter)

Peter: He was the most sophisticated guy in the FDOE. He was their lobbyist among other things and we needed to get legislation passed to enforce the decree. And he was exactly who we needed to get things for our challenges. He was about ready to retire and this was a capstone to his career. He could do something good and the guy was wonderful.

MSL: At the end of his career? That's great!

62

Peter: Yeah, then he retired and spent the rest of his days in an Airstream (chuckles).

MSL: That's great. I do have one last question for you as any good teacher education scholar would ask you and that is about the future implications of the decree, for the children of Florida? What is your hope?

Peter: Lawyers hope to change the life conditions for English Learners (ELs). Anyone who thinks a decree is a panacea hasn't been around for very long. But you hope you provide a tool that has helped kids in many places and in ways where they otherwise would not have been helped. That is my hope for the Decree.

I think down the line there are going to be more and more Latinos who are immigrants. I understand the numbers will increase and there's likely to be better implementation and more pressure to do right and so hopefully the numbers will catch up with the sentiments of the Decree and the education these kids will get improve accordingly.

MSL: That's great. I think on that note, we should probably wrap this up. Thank you!

Peter: Thank you.

CAROLYN O'GORMAN-FAZZOLARI

7. MAKING THE CLASSROOM A SPACE OF FREEDOM FOR IMMIGRANT YOUTH

Michel Foucault's research and subsequent theory of discipline and punishment asserts that society is made up of sophisticated and highly constructed forms of detainment, which are intricately and precisely developed with the explicit purpose of enforcing (and maintaining) power over the undesirable and anomalous people in society. In this chapter, the population is made up of unaccompanied immigrant minors from Central America who recently arrived to the United States. Upon crossing the U.S.-Mexican border, these minors are detained. After a period of detainment, they are placed into a sponsor's home and are required to attend school.

With this in mind, this study posits that these children circulate through a series of confinement spaces for the duration of their lives. For instance, they exit the detainment of their impoverished and gang-controlled nations and enter a physical detainment center in the United States. Then they exit the detainment center and enter the detainment of the sponsor's home. After which, they enter the detainment of the school space. Upon their exit from the school space, they enter the detainment of the workplace.

Along this circuitry of confinement, the school can potentially serve to alter the path of confinement to one of relative freedom. Thus, the pedagogical goal for educational institutions (administrators, teachers, etc.) should revolve around making the school space one that is aesthetically and structurally different from the detainment centers, as well as teaching and learning practices.

Furthermore, Foucault's (1975/1995) theory cites social workers, teachers, psychologists/therapists, the clergy, police and so on as technicians who reinforce power through the continued application of structural norms. He asserts, "As a result of this new restraint [of the body], a whole army of technicians ... [such as] wardens, doctors, chaplains, psychiatrists, psychologists, educationalists; by their very presence near the prisoner [student], they sing the praises that the law needs" (p. 11). The newly arrived immigrant minor circulates through the spaces of each supporter of the establishment of bureaucratic power. Generally, these technicians simply perform their required tasks and move the student to the next space in the circuit. To Foucault, the intent of each technician is not necessarily malicious or even conscious. The behavior of the technician has been normalized through the very systems of discipline in which the minors circulate. Foucault writes that the

M. López-Stafford Levy (Ed.), Children from the Other America, 65–81.

"practice that normalized ... by technical elaboration and rational reflection ... [is] 'normalized' (p. 295).

These structural norms include the collection of data, frequent diagnostic tests (academically/mentally/physically), placement into specific group spaces and overt enforcement of specific laws. The norms are reinforced in daily routines. Again, Foucault (1975/1995) asserts that this process serves to reinforce the power structure. He writes:

> The constitution of the individual as a describable, analyzable object in order to maintain him in his own aptitudes or abilities, under the gaze of a permanent corpus of knowledge; and, the constitution of a comparative system that made possible the measurement of groups, of collective facts, of the gaps between individuals, their distribution in a given 'population'. (p. 180)

It is significant to note that to a newly arrived person who is culturally and linguistically different faces the constant data collection and observation from the detainment center, and I argue that this carries over to the school. Hence, the minor will not detect an obvious difference between the two spaces. The data collection confines the minors, through categorization and placement, and aesthetically appears to them as monitoring and policing. Whether the data collector is a guard or a teacher, the appearance is the same.

Furthermore, the jobs of the technicians overlap to create one singular vision of constant surveillance. In describing Mattray, a penal institution for boys, Foucault (1975/1995) mentions, "The chiefs and their deputies ... had to be not exactly judges, or teachers, or foremen, or non-commissioned officers, or 'parents', but something of all these things in a quite specific mode of intervention. They were in a sense technicians of behavior: engineers of conduct, orthopaedists of individuality. Their task was to produce bodies that were both docile and capable" (p. 11). The paradoxical duties of the technicians smother the immigrant minor as they perceive this mixing of authoritative roles, but are unable to articulate how or why they operate or any identifiable difference in each one's function. Hence, to the immigrant minor they appear a kaleidoscopic continuum of incomprehensible authority.

Finally, the perpetuation of the carceral system requires the execution and participation in daily routines that reinforce the function of the structure. Foucault (1975/1995) calls this phenomenon the "micro-physics of power" (p. 26). This physical context is manifested in the strictest enforcement of the daily schedule precisely timed. The body of each immigrant minor must complete each task on time. Each task is itself precise in its formation and implementation with a series of specific rules and steps in order to complete the task. The instructors play the dual role of performing and enforcing micro-physical acts. They are at the mercy of the same institutional function. Foucault states, "the study of this micro-physics presupposes that the power exercised on the body is conceived as a strategy [with]

... a network of relations, constantly in tension, in activity ... that one should take as its model a perpetual battle rather than a contract regulating a transaction" (p. 26). In essence, a complex machinery of confinement simultaneously produces and reproduces its own power and functionality, constantly. This seemingly unstoppable force of confinement may be rational when legitimate detainment is necessary (rape, murder, Wall Street, etc.), but for the innocent immigrant minor in the physical space of the school, this method of confinement is irrational.

It can be legitimately argued that we all live in a large panoptical space of confinement. But the population under discussion carries the most severe forms of detainment. For example, according to *World Health Rankings* website, "Violence: Death Rate, 2015" section, two of the top three countries in the world with the highest rate of death by violence per 100,000 people are Guatemala and El Salvador. Most of the newly arrived immigrant minors come from these nations. Without even discussing the cause of such violence (which stems back to the Reagan period foreign policy in Central American), this population of children live in confinement in their own homes. With the addition of the border crossing and the official detainment by the United States, these children make up a group that is extra-sensitive to confinement. That is why the school is an important space that could potentially resist the microphysics of power that inertially supports confinement.

OBSERVATIONS IN THE FIELD

Listen to the stories. You want to help the world? Read the poetry of the people we're bombing. (Sherman Alexie)

With increased frequency, pleas for help (from Florida educators) started appearing on the state-wide ESOL List serve (Florida) during the 2014–2015 school year. The Central American undocumented immigrant minors were arriving at significant levels and as a result demanded attention as this "new phenomenon" took center stage. One could not help but raise an eyebrow or feel a sudden urge to help after reading and re-reading the on-line pleas. There seemed to be a sense of urgency in investigating the scope of challenges in the school spaces in order to better understand the issues from both the eyes of the adult and *especially* the newly arrived immigrant children.

I decided to visit the schools that received large numbers of students referenced in the on-line pleas. I visited specific classroom spaces and compared them aesthetically with spaces of detainment to establish the level of similarity in appearance and arrangement. Upon arriving and assessing the aesthetic layout, I proceeded to enter the classrooms where the immigrant students spent some of their time. I paid particular attention to the practices of classroom teachers to verify if their procedures served to replicate that of other detainment institutions. I also conversed with the immigrant students to better understand their narratives.

Narrative One:[1] *"The Clipboard"*

As an observer in a particular public high school classroom, I felt uncomfortable, uneasy and underprepared watching the dictatorial teacher, as she stood so erect in front of the class. It wasn't her stance so much, rather the clipboard she grasped and shifted between her arms as she glared at the students, one by one. She purposefully pointed at students, one at a time, as she so accurately placed a check mark next to certain students' names. This was apparently a gesture of classroom management, non-verbally persecuting the student, for no apparent reason. The students were not misbehaving or acting strange. In fact, they were sitting in their seats ever so obediently trying to understand the multi-step directions about how to add fancy transitions to a Power Point presentation, all in English, a language foreign to each and every student.

Apparently the check marks were strikes against the students who strayed from the expected silence or perhaps in some slight way displayed a level of discontent or readjusted the body in the hard plastic chair. The check marks and the clipboard replaced verbal communication, which didn't matter much because the students didn't understand the teacher and quite obviously, the teacher didn't understand the students. The high school students were of varied immigrant statuses, some in the country for only one month and others for a year. They announced their eagerness to learn.

"The Clipboard" Analysis

This classroom space exemplifies the power of the authority figure. With a presence of the formal guardian (like a prison guard), utilizing an instrument of data collection (the clipboard), it is impossible for the student to fully realize the school space as one of free expression and movement. Foucault (1975/1995) claims, "A general book, kept by the teachers and their assistants, recorded from day to day the behavior of the pupils and everything that happened in the school; it was periodically shown to an inspector" (p. 157). The requirement to stay seated in a micro-cell (student desk) with only minimal supplies at hand is reminiscent of the consistent lack of spacial movement and resources in previous confinement spaces. The verbal communication is without mutual comprehension. This may be an irrelevant factor, since verbal expression is discouraged for the confined minor. The verbal commands remain official and the expressions and body language, which can be utilized to calm the minor, are authoritative. The plastic institutional grade seating mirrors those in detainment centers.

Narrative Two: "The Silent 9th Grade History Text"

Second period was dreadful for the 9th grade newly arrived immigrant students. The school worked on a block schedule meaning the classes alternated days. The students had history every other day. At the beginning of each second period, the students filed into class with their hands out as if they were there to collect their daily ration of food. But it wasn't a tray. It was the ninth grade history text filled with page after page of words the students couldn't yet comprehend. They hadn't even learned survival English yet, much less American history of the military and economic events of the Civil War and Reconstruction (9th grade Florida Common Core State Standard/ CCSS).

They all knew the routine, grab the history text, move to the back of the room, open to the page number that was written on the board specifically for them, pull out a sheet of paper and start copying. Start copying, word for word, paragraph by paragraph, for the entire 80-minute period. Sometimes the bilingual paraprofessional would show up and translate a few words and that always helped. Anything would help. If the students learned two words during that 80-minute period, they were appreciative. Two words were better than none. The teacher had the students do this in class every other day. The students didn't complain; they couldn't. Instead, they were playing the role of "good student". Quiet, writing, physically present and obedient. The teacher liked that. The students took the same test as the *other* students, the English-speakers. They had to. There was no other option.

"The Silent 9th Grade History Text" Analysis

At the level of mind-numbing daily routine, this classroom epitomizes Foucault's theory. He reports, "The prison must be the microcosm of a perfect society in which individuals are isolated in their moral existence, but in which they come together in a strict hierarchical framework, with no lateral relation, communication being possible only in a vertical direction" (p. 238). Perhaps, this teacher fears a student rebellion in the space. A rebellion that consists of minors who talk, socialize, flirt, and play. But the teacher cuts off any "vertical communication" before it can occur. This is true isolation in silence. The chair is a cell of solitary confinement. The physical labor is mundane, unending, and continuous. Most of all it serves no other purpose than to dehumanize and to produce the docile body. This is preparation for future labor where demeaning repetitive tasks performed under the supervision of a monolingual authority figure is normalized.

DISCUSSION AND IMPLICATIONS FOR PRACTICE

According to the U.S. Department of Education (2015) website, under the "Laws and Guidance/Civil Rights: Educational Services for Immigrant Children and Those Recently Arrived to the United States" section, unaccompanied immigrant minors who arrive at the U.S.-Mexican border from Central America are entitled to equal access to a public elementary and secondary education, regardless of their or their parents' actual or perceived national origin, citizenship, or immigration status. This includes minors who are in immigration proceedings while residing in local communities with a parent, family member, or other appropriate adult sponsor. Simply put, the minors are processed upon arriving at the border, are then detained for up to 35 days in a U.S. Department of Health and Human Services (HHS) non-profit shelter while authorities locate a sponsor, are processed again upon confirmation of reuniting with the sponsor and then released. These minors are required to be fully enrolled in a public school while they continue to be processed for immigration purposes.

In the case of some Florida schools, from the moment the students enter the school space, they are directed to comply with the standardized "rigorous monolingual English curriculum" that is offered in each of their high school classes. In-class observations and informal conversations with the students revealed the glaring contradictions of "equal access" to a public education and particularly "rigorous" teaching and learning. For example, in one high school class, the students' academic task for the day was to copy isolated words from the thematic English picture dictionary. That day's theme was "The Farm" (farmer, tractor, corn stalk, barn, silo...). The other teaching professional ("The Clipboard" narrative) had the newly arrived immigrant high school students listening to a video on how to add transitions to a Power Point presentation. That seemed to engage the students to a higher degree but what troubled me, and the students, was the teacher's policing of behavior to the extent that I, the observer, the visitor, felt fearful.

Furthermore, on one of the high school visits, I was asked by a non-Spanish-speaking teacher to directly ask the immigrant students (in Spanish), "Who is responsible for your learning?" and "If you don't learn English, who is responsible for that?" In other words, who is to blame if they do not learn the selected monolingual English curriculum, which strongly implies zero tolerance for native tongue language use in and around the classroom or school? I found this question to be extremely inappropriate and even disturbing to ask. As a result, the dialogue with the group of students wavered, while flashes of pre-service teacher program training numbed my thought process. This was a question reserved for student teachers studying Bloom's work, not a group of recently arrived immigrant students who just trekked thousands of miles and were recently released from the sterile confines of holding centers and detainment. This question reinforces the inappropriate measures imposed on these students. Was this teacher inadvertently expressing her inability to reach and teach the students or was this teacher reaching and searching for ways to understand her students' psyches based on a self-identification of failing to teach?

Simple logic tells us that students from a culturally and linguistically diverse land realize a vast array of challenges when forced to remain obedient in an educational mechanism that exclusively uses the majority language in the confines of the educational institution and enacts wildly gross expectations taken straight from the dominant ideological "handbook" of the dominant culture. The resulting impediment lies in the immigrant students' inability to express their true sense of self, character and intellect. The observed actions of the immigrant students in that particular high school resembled those of puppet students, similar to those trained to high levels of obedience, principally because the high school courses offered did not match the students' academic and educational needs, making them additional statistics to the numbers of perpetual failures in U.S. schools.

WORDS CONCERNING CRITICAL CLASSROOM LIBERATION FROM A BILINGUAL TEACHER

One approach to classroom teaching involves clearing the assumed mechanisms of control out of the teaching and learning space. Through an overt critical engagement of the systems of power with the students, a liberated classroom space can develop. An appropriate starting point for this teacher objective is to imagine the classroom in its most basic form. One can look to Jean Paul Sartre's *Existential is a Humanism* speech for a philosophical basis for clearing the space. According to Sartre (1946/2007), "there is at least one being whose existence comes before its essence, a being which exists before it can be defined by any conception of it. That being is man". So existence precedes essence. When this basic premise of existentialism is applied to the classroom, a new foundation for approaching the interaction of teacher and students comes into view. For example, rather than seeing the institutionalization of the classroom space as part of the broad bureaucratic network of hierarchal accountability, one can strip down the idea of the classroom to its existential base. That base being that an adult person will meet with several children at the same time in the same place to interact with the intent of learning something. With this existential approach, all of the institutional and bureaucratic variables that cloud the simple fact of people meeting to learn are eliminated.

This idea includes the removal of terms like "teacher" and "student." It removes the ingrained concepts related to the spatial arrangements of the class. It negates the artificial urgency related to State and Federal requirements. Sartre continues, "He will be what he makes of himself. Thus, there is no human nature" (p. 22). The meeting space is what the human adult makes of it and the communication of information is open to what the participants make it. Sartre uses the terms "human nature." Applied to the classroom, human nature represents the idea of the legally rigid and fixed space with further legal requirements in curriculum and testing. The teacher may view these requirements as natural and as if ordained by a god like figure. Of course, that god like figure is a vast network of professionals in a hierarchal arrangement. The reality is that nothing is natural about the current arrangement of the classroom as dictated by the power elite. So the teacher is free to see the interaction within the space as simple as what it actually is: people meeting to learn. This liberates the teacher and the teacher can make a space of her own creation. This requires that the teacher implements heart-felt well-researched critical interaction.

In theory this idea sounds empowering, but in practice, it is far more difficult to manifest. For example, a recent interview with a 4th grade dual language teacher illustrates the real dynamics of classroom freedom and student "achievement." This teacher does her best to employ an existential teaching foundation and chooses to subvert the institutional mandates.

What level of freedom do you feel that you have in your job?

My building principal is able to allow me the latitude to continue using best practices for English Language Learners because my NWEA growth scores exceed expectations each year. For the moment, I feel I am "getting away with" doing right by my students. Were there a different principal, I doubt that even my growth scores would keep the crushing oppressiveness of corporate education "reform" at bay. I will not conform and expect to quickly lose my job if the current principal finds employment elsewhere.

In your opinion, do you feel other teachers would agree or disagree with you? My peers indicate that they are literally afraid not to teach in the lockstep dictated by the system. They are in a vicious, unbroken cycle from which they see no reprieve. The only disagreement from them would be in the form of them seeing no latitude or freedom what-so-ever and believing that they must conform to often conflicting guidelines, paired with impossible expectations, which leave them feeling hopeless and helpless. They keep doing exactly as they are told, even though they know that documented academic failure will be the result. They believe that doing exactly as they are told will somehow protect their jobs. The irony is that in doing exactly as they are told, they ensure that their students are not able to make the necessary growth each year, per the very reliably accurate, bottom up and self-adjusting NWEA assessment.

Can you give some examples?

After administering Pearson Vue's PARCC assessment I felt like I needed a brown armband. With no prompt from me, a fellow teacher volunteered that she felt like she needed a brown armband …as though we were blindly following a Nazi regime. I instructed both classes of my dual language students to not take the PARCC seriously. I explained that there were going to be many questions that were impossible and not to allow those questions to cause them to feel stupid. I told them the authors of the test are the ones who are stupid, and that they are actually complete idiots, working for a multinational British based company, who clearly have no clue about the concept of brain development in children. Next, I explained brain development and pointed out exactly what types of math problems on the PARCC sample test would be impossible for them to understand at their ages. I also informed them about the United Opt Out

Movement web page and told them that their parents have the right to refuse this type of testing. Least they forget, I have a United Opt Out automobile window sticker, which is visible from the school playground, next to which I park daily. In my room the very subject of the PARCC and everything I am expected to do leading up to it was a very teachable moment and provoked thoughtful classroom discussion. I used it in the only useful way I could muster.

In other rooms, where teachers did not risk speaking out like this, some students vomited from stress. In the classroom next door to me, some students wrote, "I'm stupid" over and over on their tests. Of course, the teacher next door to me was risking her job by admitting that she witnessed this, as we are not allowed to look at the questions on the test.

The interview exemplifies how the countless inclusion of unrelenting interference of needless institutional regulations obscures the basic existential interaction of human beings. A series of procedures and statutes mediates the teacher's interaction with the students. This creates an atmosphere of stress and fear for all the humans involved, teacher or students. In this climate of stress and fear, it proves impossible to manifest the kind of individual creative force required for the best possible classroom communication and collaboration. For instance, job security appears to be a major concern for teachers. With the fear of losing one's means of sustenance, the teacher, against their intrinsic judgment reproduces the fear of failure. The above example shows that teachers can rebel and create their own spaces of free association with the students. Sartre (1946/2007) states, "And, when we say that man is responsible for himself, we do not mean that he is responsible only for his own individuality, but that he is responsible for all men" (p. 23). So when the teacher decides to capture the classroom space, she/he captures that space for all teachers. Finally, the classrooms which include the newly arrived Central American immigrant minors is a particularly vulnerable space because these students do not have the resources or advocates outside of the classroom (such as parents) to ensure the appropriate classroom practices are in place. That is why it is up to the teacher to critically teach these students without imposing the inappropriate institutional restrictions upon them.

PLAN TO FREE THE SPACE

Rationale

The following collection of transformational considerations for educators serves to unravel the elements of detainment that boldly restrict teachers from liberating themselves, their students, their instructional spaces, and their freedom to practice. In an attempt to demolish the prevalent and obvious confinement practices within our classrooms and schools, we must work toward a complete shift in how we think about, negotiate, and transform the relationship among classroom teaching, the production of knowledge, the institutional structures of the school, and the social and material relations of the wider community, society, and nation-state. We must avoid a "reactionary" response to fixing the problems and addressing the challenges (McLaren, 2000, p. 35). In other words, we must inject our daily practices with the fundamental aspects of critical pedagogy.

The outlined considerations, with roots in critical pedagogy, highlight a short list of theoretical, practical and reflective considerations for working with recently arrived immigrant students in local contexts. It must first be understood that, "In the process of becoming fully human, everyday life must be informed by a theory and practice relationship that truly alters ideas and experience within a larger revolutionary dialectic" (McLaren, 2000, p. 202). Further, the considerations serve to promote thought markers, that are alive and productive, and that when contemplated singularly or collectively ignite actions toward liberating the learning space with conscious forming *praxis*, or the constant reciprocity of theory and practice. Theory building and critical reflection inform our practice and our action, and our practice and action inform our theory building and critical reflection (Wink, 2005, p. 50).

PLAN TO FREE THE SPACE:
CONSIDERATIONS FOR TRANSFORMATIVE PRACTICE

Schools are places where, as part of civil society, spaces of uncoerced interaction can be created. (McLaren on Freire, 2000)

Academic/Curricular:

- An "emancipatory" approach to curricular studies emphasizes "critical reflection" on one's own "concrete situation". A "problem-posing" method requires "dialogue" in which teacher and students are "critical coinvestigators". They both "develop their power to perceive critically the way they exist in the world with which and in which they find themselves; they come to see the world not as a static reality, but as a reality in process, in transformation" (as cited in Posner, 1998, p. 93).

- Academic engagement for academic success is connected to what the students are learning, how they are learning it, and who they are learning it with (Suárez-Orozco, Suárez-Orozco & Todorova, 2008).
- Are we confident that we have a comprehensive understanding of our students' aptitude for intellectual work and their subsequent achievement based in critical learning?

Care/Caring:

- Caring Theory addresses the need for pedagogy to follow from and flow through relationships cultivated between teacher and student. Although *educación* has implications for pedagogy, it is first a foundational cultural construct that provides instructions on how one should live in the world. With its emphasis on respect, responsibility, and sociality, it provides a benchmark against which all humans are to be judged, formally educated or not. (Valenzuela, 1999, p. 21)
- "What does it mean to care about children from marginalized communities, given the political and social context in which education takes place?" (Valenzuela, 1999, p. xvi)

Courage:

- "To fight and to love" (Freire, 2005, p. 75).
- Courage, as a virtue, is not something I can find outside myself. Because it comprises the conquering of my fears, it implies fear. First of all, in speaking about fear we must make sure that we are speaking of something very concrete. In other words, fear is not an abstraction. Second, we must make sure that we understand that we are speaking of something very normal. And, when we speak about fear, we are faced with the need to be very clear about our choices, and that requires certain concrete procedures and practices, which are the very experiences that cause fear (p. 75).
- When we are faced with concrete fears, such as that of losing our jobs or of not being promoted, we feel that need to set certain limits to our fear. Before anything else, we begin to recognize that fear is a manifestation of our being alive. But I must not allow my fears to immobilize me. If I am secure in my political dream, having tactics that may lesson risk, I must go on with the fight. Hence, the need to be in control of my fear, to *educate* my fear, from which is finally born my courage (p. 75).
- How will we be collectively courageous today in building a sustained liberated learning environment?

Critical Reflection:

- Reflection circulates within discourse as a multiple learning event. Freire (1998) claims, "For this reason, in the process of the ongoing education of teachers, the essential moment is that of critical reflection on one's practice. Thinking critically about practice, of today or yesterday makes possible the improvement of tomorrow's practice" (p. 45–46). If we do not daily reflect on our pedagogical practice, the negative experiences exponentially add up until every day is negative. This danger causes a demoralization that leads to pessimism. Once the pessimism sets in, ideas of personal hope and optimism become more and more difficult to initiate. For example, critical reflection on the classroom space within the context of confinement may lead to altering the space.
- What does it mean to critically reflect rather than just reflect on one's practice?
- How can we offer opportunities for students to critically reflect?

Democracy:

- A democratic community must, accordingly, enable people (students) to develop values and ideas that outline alternative possibilities. Equally important, such a community must generate concrete practices that enact a moral vision- a vision not reducible to any set of present realities and yet not simply an Idealist construction. A democratic community encourages its members to become participants in civic discussions that require concerted, collaborative actions in the name of social justice and structural change (Beyer, 1998, p. 257–258).
- Advocacy for disenfranchised groups (McLaren, 2000, p. 175).
- Embrace a pedagogy of hope, whereby "students are invited to discover for themselves the nature of democracy and its functioning," whereby students move from their object positions as they become agents of history in a constant quest for the truth (Chomsky, 2000, p. 12).
- How can the learning environment help to nurture a democratic space that serves to break down the harmful forces of marginalization? (Wink, 2005, p. 122)

Dialectic:

- A dialectic involves seeing and articulating contradictions; it is the process of learning from the oppositional view. A dialectic brings to light a more comprehensive understanding of the multiple facets of the opposite. As we learn while teaching (each other) and teach while learning (from one another), we are in a dialectical process (Wink, 2005, p. 41).
- Addresses the tensions between opposing thoughts, ideals, values, and beliefs (p. 41).
- This fully relates to confinement and opens the conversation that concerns the classroom as well as the school space. Countless questions can be discussed about every contradictory aspect of the school and education, in general.

Identity:

- "Let's think a little about the learners' cultural identity and about the respect that we owe it in our educational practice" (Freire, 2005, p. 127).
- When immigrant students feel that their intelligence, imagination and multilingual talents are affirmed in the school and classroom context, they invest their identities much more actively in the learning process (Cummins, 2009, p. 32).
- Identity grows and changes because of context. We must recognize that fixed definitions of identity can be problematic. Therefore, a foundation of love and respect should foreground any concept and practice related to identity.
- Do we support the development of the identity without interference or are we promoting identity to the point where students feel compelled to conform to either what their identities are supposed to be or to the dominant cultural identity? Freire (1998) notes, "those who are different from us always requires of us a large dose of humility that would alert us to the risks of overvaluing our identity, which could, on the one hand, turn into a form of arrogance and, on the other, promote the devaluation of other human beings" (p. 111).

Historical Context:

- Historical Context represents one of the most critical aspects related to newly arrived Central American minors. We must take the time to do a comprehensive study of the history in that region, particularly as it relates to the United States' involvement in the region. An honest study leaves us with a more complete answer to the question: Why are they coming? If we understand the historical context, then explanations of North American exceptionalism as the reason for this wave of immigration, appears hollow. Also, the oversimplified explanation of violence, etc. is equally hollow.
- Why are they really coming?

Human Capital:

- The students arrive with a wealth of human capital. We must create a space where their cultural capital is valued. They arrive with experiences that school technicians have and will never face. They enter after having overcome challenges that far exceed any challenge related to educating the students. Freire (1998) asks, "Why not discuss with the students the concrete reality of their lives and that aggressive reality in which violence is permanent and where people are much more familiar with death than with life? Why not establish an "intimate" connection between knowledge considered basic curriculum and knowledge that is the fruit of the lived experience of these students as individuals?" (p. 38).
- Develop a critical comprehension of psychological entities such as "memories, beliefs, values, meanings, and so forth…which are actually out in the social world of action and interaction" (as cited in Chomsky, 2000, p. 11). We must first read

the world – the cultural, social, and political practices that constitute it – before we can make sense of the word-level description of reality (Chomsky, 2000).

- How can I honor the students' lived experiences and afford the students the opportunity to study the lives of people like themselves and the forces that shape those lives? (Gabbard, 2003, p. 69)
- How will we embed the students' native culture (and language) into the learning environment?

Language:

- Multiple Multilingual Education emphasizes multiplicity in the use of more than two autonomous separate languages in instruction and the intertwining of the language practices, including translanguaging (García, 2009, p. 149).
- Dynamic bilingualism/multilingualism is the goal. This refers to language practices that are multiple and ever adjusting to the multilingual multimodal terrain of the communicative act (p. 144).
- How can the students begin and continue to build on their heteroglossic language practices (a product of lived multilingual experiences)? (p. 149)

Liberation:

- Understand and practice the move from the liberal humanist notion of "traditional democratic freedom" to that of freeing oneself and others from the relation of the dialectical contradiction (McLaren on Freire, 2000, p. 175).
- Education and cultural processes aimed at liberation do not succeed by freeing people from their chains, but by preparing them collectively to free themselves. This is dialectically facilitated when conversation is replaced by a dialogical praxis. We need to restore to liberation its rightful place as the central project of education (p. 175).
- How can we honestly learn to free our learning and loving space in the name of education?

Literacy:

- Literacy does not grow in isolation; rather, literate processes grow from families, from schools, from work, from cultures, from knowledges, from technologies (Wink, 2005, p. 47), from languages, translanguaging, and crossing borders. Critical literacy recognizes that reading does not take place in a vacuum; it includes the entire social, cultural, political, and historical context.
- "It doesn't matter *what* you read, what matters is *how* you read it. Now, I don't mean to comic books, but there's a lot of cultural wealth out there from all over the place, and to learn what it means to be culturally rich, you can explore almost anywhere: there's no fixed subset that is the basis of truth and understanding." (Chomsky, 2003, p. 27).

- How can we promote critical literacy skills in all languages including transfer of knowledge from one language to the next?

Revolutionary Pedagogy:

- Cultivated from a shared history of struggle, a struggle conjugated with hope, infused with revolutionary love, and dignified by a great exertion of the ethical imagination and human will and its infusion into the struggle for social justice (McLaren, 2000, p. 202).
- *Integration* with one's context, as distinguished from *adaption*, is a distinctively human activity. Integration results from the capacity to adapt oneself to reality *plus* the critical capacity to make choices and to transform that reality. To the extent that man loses his ability to make choices and is subjected to the choices of others, to the extent that his decision are no longer his own because they result from external prescriptions, he is no longer integrated. Rather, he has adapted. He has "adjusted." Unpliant men, with a revolutionary spirit, are often termed "maladjusted" (Freire, 1974, p. 4).
- How will the students be fully integrated into the educational context to make personal critical choices?

Social Justice:

- Value the strength of immigrant students and communities, and build on their language practices. Enable the creation of learning contexts that are not threatening to the students' identities, while maintaining academic rigor and upholding high expectations (García, 2009).
- Social justice education for immigrant students means having the same value put on the students' language, culture, ideas, customs, intellects, interests, and values as is put on all other students (non-immigrant students). It is a non-judgmental, celebratory, inclusive type of education (Hawkins, 2011).
- How can I advocate for the linguistic, cultural and academic human rights of my students?

Social Responsibility:

- Emphasizes exchange networks of trust and solidarity among students wishing to attain goals that cannot be individually attained. The composite imagery of caring that unfolds accords moral authority to teachers and institutional structures that value and actively promote respect and a search for connection, particularly among students themselves (Valenzuela, 1999, p. 21).
- To educate the child to make him a useful member of society. It is their [the Socialists'] purpose that the schools shall equip the children to cope with their environment and to bring out the best that is in them- not by grinding them through an educational mill as sausages are ground from a machine, but by giving

the individual opportunity to develop to his fullest capacity in the direction that his talents are most promising. But in giving the individual opportunity, at the same time they recognize the need for cultivating social consciousness and community spirit (*Milwaukee Leader* editorial, March 19, 1923, as cited in Teitelbaum, 1998, p. 39).

• How will I support my community of learners to ensure that their best interests are being served?

CONCLUSION

The narratives presented in the study illustrate one of the central issues facing the education of the newly arrived Central American immigrant minors. This study demonstrates the level of control placed upon the teacher and, subsequently, upon the students by the teacher. Foucault's (1975/1995) statement that "The perpetual penality that traverses all points and supervises every instant in the disciplinary institutions compares, differentiates, hierarchizes, homogenizes and excludes. In short, it normalizes" (p. 183). Foucault's statement applies to teachers and students. Once the classroom teacher is normalized by pre-service teacher training programs and directives to conform, it becomes all the harder to liberate. At the core of the entire educational structure there exists constant oversight that inhibits the ability of teachers to create their classrooms. Because the institutions mandate subservience to procedure, curriculum, and assessment, those within the classroom are under tremendous pressure to abide. Fundamentally, the possibility for positive change lies in the hands of the classroom teacher. Teachers must reflect on the level of constraints imposed upon them and make clear decisions informed by the drive to liberate themselves. Once teachers liberate themselves, they can, in turn, liberate these confined students. Perhaps teachers can look at this moment as their own dangerous trek through the desert to a place of freedom and possibility.

NOTE

[1] The narratives are written in an informal tone as a stylistic choice in order to emphasize the general mood of the classroom space.

REFERENCES

Beyer, L. (1998). Schooling for democracy. In L. Beyer & M. Apple (Eds.), *The curriculum: Problems, politics, and possibilities* (pp. 245–263). Albany, NY: State University of New York Press.

Chomsky, N. (2000). *Chomsky on miseducation.* New York, NY: Rowman & Littlefield.

Chomsky, N. (2003). The function of schools: Subtler and cruder methods of control. In K. Saltman & D. Gabbard (Eds.), *Education as enforcement: The militarization and corporatization of schools* (pp. 25–35). New York, NY: RoutledgeFalmer.

Cummins, J. (2009). Fundamental psycholinguistic and sociological principles underlying educational success for linguistic minority students. In T. Skutnabb-Kangas, R. Phillispson, A. Mohanty, & M. Panda (Eds.), *Social justice through multilingual education* (pp. 19–35). Buffalo, NY: Multilingual Matters.

Foucault, M. (1995). *Discipline and punish: The birth of the prison* (A. Sheridan, Trans.). New York, NY: Vintage Books. (Original work published 1975)

Freire, P. (1974). *Education for critical consciousness.* New York, NY: Bloomsbury.

Freire, P. (1998). *Pedagogy of freedom, ethics, democracy and civic courage.* Lanham: MD: Rowman & Littlefield.

Freire, P. (2005). *Teachers as cultural workers: Letters to those who dare teach.* Boulder, CO: Westview Press.

Gabbard, D. (2003). The function of schools: Subtler and cruder methods of control. In K. Saltman & D. Gabbard (Eds.), *Education as enforcement: The militarization and corporatization of schools* (pp. 61–78). New York, NY: RoutledgeFalmer.

García, O. (2009). Education, multilingualism and translanguaging in the 21st century. In T. Skutnabb-Kangas, R. Phillispson, A. Mohanty, & M. Panda (Eds.), *Social justice through multilingual education* (pp. 19–35). Buffalo, NY: Multilingual Matters.

Hawkins, M. (2011). Dialogic determination: Constructing a social justice discourse in language teacher education. In M. Hawkins (Ed.), *Social justice language teacher education* (pp. 102–123). Buffalo, NY: Multilingual Matters.

McLaren, P. (2000). *Che Guevara, Paulo Freire, and the pedagogy of revolution.* New York, NY: Rowman & Littlefield Publishers, Inc.

Orozco-Suárez, C., Orozco-Suárez, M., & Todorova, I. (2008). *Learning a new land: Immigrant students in American schools.* Cambridge, MA: Belknap Press of Harvard University Press.

Posner, G. (1998). Models of curriculum planning. In L. Beyer & M. Apple (Eds.), *The curriculum: Problems, politics, and possibilities* (pp. 79–100). Albany, NY: State University of New York Press.

Sartre, J. (2007). *Existentialism is a humanism; Including, a commentary on the stranger* (C. Macomber, Trans.) New Haven, CT: Yale University Press. (Original work published 1946)

Teitelbaum, K. (1998). Contestation and curriculum: The efforts of American Socialists, 1900–1920. In L. Beyer & M. Apple (Eds.), *The curriculum: Problems, politics, and possibilities* (pp. 34–57). Albany, NY: State University of New York Press.

U.S. Department of Education Website. (2015). *Laws and guidance – Civil rights: Educational services for immigrant children and those recently arrived to the United States.* Retrieved from http://www2.ed.gov/policy/rights/guid/unaccompanied-children.html

Valenzuela, A. (1999). *Subtractive schooling: U.S.-Mexican youth and politics of caring.* Albany, NY: State University of Ney York Press.

Violence: Death Rate per 100,000 Age Standardized. (2015). *World health rankings.* Retrieved from http://www.worldlifeexpectancy.com/cause-of-death/violence/by-country/

JEFF DUNCAN-ANDRADE

8. ROSE IN THE CONCRETE[1]

NOTE TO EDUCATORS: HOPE REQUIRED WHEN GROWING
ROSES IN CONCRETE

The idea that hope alone will transform the world, and action undertaken in that kind of naïveté, is an excellent route to hopelessness, pessimism, and fatalism. But the attempt to do without hope, in the struggle to improve the world, as if that struggle could be reduced to calculated acts alone, or a purely scientific approach, is a frivolous illusion. (Freire, 1997, p. 8)

Barack Obama's presidential campaign positioned him as the leader who could help restore hope to the nation. Drawing heavily from his widely read memoir *The Audacity of Hope* (2006), the campaign used hope as a core principle around which Obama laid out his vision for "reclaiming the American dream." However, Obama was not the first to use a framework of hope to generate social movement. Historically, hope has been a theme in the lives and movements of the poor and dispossessed in the United States. During the civil rights era, as well as other key historical moments of social change, the nation's hope connected moral outrage to action aimed at resolving undeserved suffering.

In the past three decades, however, there has been an assault on hope, particularly in our nation's urban centers. This attack has taken place on numerous fronts, including disinvestment in schools and overinvestment in a prison industrial complex. Such policies have eroded true hope and given rise to false hope, a reactionary distortion of the radical premise of hope. Therefore, this essay begins by cautioning educators against three types of false hope often promulgated in urban schools: hokey hope, mythical hope, and hope deferred.

The second half of this essay attends to the work of educators in rebuilding the critical hope that has been worn down in our communities. Such educators deliver us from false hope by teaching in ways that connect the moral outrage of young people to actions that relieve the undeserved suffering in their communities. The spread of this kind of educational practice in our schools adds to hopefulness because it develops a transgenerational capacity for long-term, sustainable, critical hope in communities. Brazilian critical educator Paulo Freire (1997) described this kind of hope as an "ontological need," especially in the lives and the pedagogy of educators

M. López-Stafford Levy (Ed.), Children from the Other America, 83–95.
© *2009. Boston: Harvard University. Reprinted with permission.*

working in communities where forms of social misery seem to have taken up permanent residence. And so, on the heels of a hope-filled, history-making election that comes sixteen years into my calling as an urban schoolteacher, I also wish to share some reflections on three elements of educational practice that can build and sustain critical hope in urban schools.

ENEMIES OF HOPE

Hokey Hope Optimism, Cornel West (2004) argues, "adopts the role of the spectator who surveys the evidence in order to infer that things are going to get better" (p. 296), even when the evidence does not warrant such a conclusion. This hokey hope is peddled in urban schools all the time. It is akin to what Martin Luther King Jr. (1963) referred to as "the tranquilizing drug of gradualism" (para. 5): an individualistic up-by-your-bootstraps hyperbole that suggests if urban youth just work hard, pay attention, and play by the rules, then they will go to college and live out the "American dream." I do not condemn this false hope because I doubt the importance of time and hard work for creating change. Rather, this hope is "hokey" because it ignores the laundry list of inequities that impact the lives of urban youth long before they get to the under-resourced schools that reinforce an uneven playing field.

Angela Valenzuela's Subtractive Schooling (1999) provides a profound examination of how hokey hope is manifested in Seguin High School, a predominantly Latino school in Texas. She argues that Seguin is indicative of a national culture of ineffective schools that is "structured around an aesthetic caring whose essence lies in an attention to things and ideas" (p. 22). Relationships between school officials and students become pragmatic, the teaching and learning process is strained, and an "impersonal and objective language, including such terms as goals, strategies, and standardized curricula, is used in decisions made by one group for another" (p. 22). This leads to a culture of false caring, one in which the more powerful members of the relationship define themselves as caring despite the fact that the recipients of their so-called caring do not perceive it as such. Valenzuela's aesthetically caring teachers drew heavily from the work-ethic rhetoric to describe "good" students and doled out care in proportion to students' willingness to be accommodating of an unjust society and an unequal school.

Ultimately, hokey hope projects some kind of multicultural, middle-class opportunity structure that is inaccessible to the overwhelming majority of working-class, urban youth of color. This, in turn, largely delegitimizes the pain that urban youth experience as a result of a persistently unequal society. It is a false hope informed by privilege and rooted in the optimism of the spectator who needs not suffer—a "let them eat cake" utterance that reveals a fundamental incomprehension of suffering.

MYTHICAL HOPE

Obama's election has the potential to contribute to mythical hope, what Roland Barthes (1972) might have described as a false narrative of equal opportunity emptied of its historical and political contingencies. The significance of the election of a black man as the president of this country is undeniable, especially given our past and present national failure to meet the challenge of racial equality. But immediately after an election that few would have predicted, the overstatement of its significance began; it became naturalized as the consequence of a fictitious color-blind society. In John McCain's (2008) concession speech, after referencing the white rage that followed Booker T. Washington's dinner with President Theodore Roosevelt at the White House in 1901, McCain proclaimed:

> America today is a world away from the cruel and prideful bigotry of that time. There is no better evidence of this than the election of an African American to the presidency of the United States. Let there be no reason now for any American to fail to cherish their citizenship in this, the greatest nation on Earth. (para. 6)

McCain's insinuation that this election signifies the "end of racism" (D'Souza, 1995) is mythmaking. His statement ignores the fact that people of color trail their white counterparts on virtually every indicator of social, political, and economic well-being. Educators must not use Obama's election as evidence that we have emerged victorious in our battle with racism or with any of the oppressions (classism, patriarchy, xenophobia, homophobia) that continue to cripple our society. Obama (2006) himself preempted this argument by pointing out:

> To say that we are one people is not to suggest that race no longer matters... To suggest that our racial attitudes play no part in ... disparities is to turn a blind eye to both our history and our experience—and to relieve ourselves of the responsibility to make things right. (pp. 232–233)

Perhaps this is why West (2008) describes Obama's election as sitting precariously between an example of the American dream coming true and "the grand exhaustion of the dream built on the success of any one individual" (pp. 58–59). Educators must understand that Obama's election gives us "hope on a tightrope," because a single event cannot, by itself, provide the healing and long-term sustenance required to maintain hope amid conditions of suffering. Obama's election is change, and he may even give us some reason to be hopeful. Time will tell. But he neither embodies nor can he produce a fundamental departure from the inequities our children experience in the classroom. No president, no policy, and no program can do this for us. To claim otherwise is to peddle a mythical hope.

Mythical hope is a profoundly ahistorical and depoliticized denial of suffering that is rooted in celebrating individual exceptions. These individuals are used to construct a myth of meritocracy that simultaneously fetishizes them as objects of that myth. Ultimately, mythical hope depends on luck and the law of averages to produce individual exceptions to the tyranny of injustice, and thus it denies the legitimacy of the suffering of the oppressed. Educators must avoid the trap of overstating the significance of Obama's election for teaching and learning in urban schools, because, at the end of the day, we are the ones who create classrooms that instill in our young people the "audacity to hope" (Wright, 1990).

HOPE DEFERRED

Hope deferred, constructed on a progressive politics of despair, is a common justification for poor teaching. It hides behind misinterpretations of research that connect the material conditions of poverty to the constraints placed on schools. Many teachers feel overwhelmed by the challenges urban youth face in their lives and consider themselves ill-equipped to respond with a pedagogy that will develop hope in the face of such daunting hardships. They are liberal-minded enough to avoid "blaming the victim," turning instead to blaming the economy, the violence in society, the lack of social services, the "system." These teachers have a critique of social inequality but cannot manifest this critique in any kind of transformative pedagogical project (Solórzano & Delgado-Bernal, 2001). They "hope" for change in its most deferred forms: either a collective utopia of a future reformed society or, more often, the individual student's future ascent to the middle class.

However, according to S. Leonard Syme (2004), professor emeritus at the University of California, Berkeley School of Public Health, hope should be thought of as "control of destiny" (p. 3), an actively present sense of agency to manage the immediate stressors in one's daily life. He argues that recent research into the importance of hope for life outcomes is a "major breakthrough in thinking" for scholars in public health and epidemiology (p. 3). Syme attributes the genesis of this breakthrough to the groundbreaking Whitehall studies, which led to revelations that the distribution of "virtually every disease in every industrialized country in the world" (p. 3) was remarkably well-correlated with social class. For a growing number of scholars, the most likely explanation for the unequal distribution of health is the unequal distribution of hope along the social gradient.

At the bottom of this social gradient, where urban youth are positioned, this "control of destiny" is almost nonexistent. David Williams, of the Harvard School of Public Health, argues that this results in the

> accumulation of multiple negative stressors, and it's so many of them it's as if someone is being hit from every single side. And, it's not only that they are dealing with a lot of stress, [it's that] they have few resources to cope. (Adelman, 2008)

The exposure to chronic stress associated with living in these types of "socially toxic environments" (Garbarino, 1995) is now thought of as one of the most—if not the most—significant contributors to poor health. This research helps us understand that many of the health problems plaguing poor communities result from "unnatural causes" (Adelman, 2008), confirming what we have known intuitively for years: inequality is making us sick.

The implications of chronic stress for teaching and learning are profound. Consider Abraham Maslow's (1943) hierarchy of needs, which defined a person's primary human needs (food, clothing, shelter, and safety) as prerequisites for pursuing needs higher up on the scale (such as education). When we connect the dots between Maslow's framework and the latest research on inequality, a serious dilemma is revealed for urban youth whose exposure to unremitting stressors leaves most, sometimes all, of their primary human needs under constant attack. When we are unwilling to confront these harsh realities of social inequality with our pedagogy—to cultivate their "control of destiny"—all we have left to offer youth is hope deferred. This offer comes when we ask our students to set their sights on some temporally distant (and highly unlikely) future well-being. There is nothing wrong with setting long-term goals with students, but hope deferred advocates that students take a path that the educator is unwilling to help them find. This student path is almost always individualistic in nature and requires a level of sacrifice that most teachers themselves are loath to make. Eventually students come to perceive a significant gap between their most pressing needs and the education we offer them. When they figure out that the teacher is unwilling and/or unable to close this gap, their hope is deferred. And just as Martin Luther King Jr. foretold of justice, hope too long deferred is hope denied.

CRITICAL HOPE: THE ENEMY OF HOPELESSNESS

On the flipside of these false hopes lies critical hope, which rejects the despair of hopelessness and the false hopes of "cheap American optimism" (West, 2008, p. 41). Critical hope demands a committed and active struggle "against the evidence in order to change the deadly tides of wealth inequality, group xenophobia, and personal despair" (West, 2004, pp. 296–297). There are three elements of critical hope: material, Socratic, and audacious. Unlike the forms of false hope, which can operate independent of one another, these three elements of critical hope must operate holistically and, in fact, are mutually constitutive. I have wrestled them apart only for the purpose of analytic convenience.

Tupac Shakur (1999) referred to young people who emerge in defiance of socially toxic environments as the "roses that grow from concrete." Concrete is one of the worst imaginable surfaces in which to grow, devoid of essential nutrients and frequently contaminated by pollutants. Any growth in such an environment is painful because all of the basic requirements for healthy development (sun, water, and nutrient-rich soil) must be hard-won. The ability to control, in a material way, the litany of social stressors that result from growing up in concrete is nearly impossible for urban youth. Educators committed to material hope engage their work by tempering this reality with the acknowledgment that there are always cracks in concrete. The quality of our teaching, along with the resources and networks we connect our students to, are those cracks. They do not create an ideal environment for growth, but they afford some leaking in of sunlight, water, and other resources that provide the material justification to hope. The courage to pursue the painful path of bursting through those jagged cracks in the concrete is what I call Socratic hope. The solidarity to share in others' suffering, to sacrifice self so that other roses may bloom, to collectively struggle to replace the concrete completely with a rose garden is what I call audacious hope. The following sections discuss each of these elements in turn.

MATERIAL HOPE

Material hope is one element of the critical hope that teachers can cultivate in their students, and it comes from the sense of control young people have when they are given the resources to "deal with the forces that affect their lives" (Syme, 2004, p. 3). It seems like a simple point, but teachers who want to build material hope must understand that quality teaching is the most significant "material" resource they have to offer youth. The best of the research in our field defines "quality" in teaching by our ability to produce student growth across assessment measures (grades, social development, test scores, student engagement, etc.). To accomplish this, we have to bust the false binary that suggests we must choose between an academically rigorous pedagogy and one geared toward social justice. An English teacher participating in my three-year study of successful urban educators in Los Angeles put it this way:

> Terms are not difficult to teach. The question, really, is will you take the time to make the things you teach relevant to students? The terms I teach are present in students' lives every day. But most people try to teach them strictly by using textbooks, worksheets, or the literature. I teach them using life and then it's much easier for students to connect them to what they are reading.[2]

The most effective urban educators, in every discipline at every grade level, connect the academic rigor of content areas with their students' lives (Duncan-Andrade, 2007). If we are serious about giving our children hope, we must reflect on how to connect our pedagogy to the harsh realities of poor, urban communities. An e-mail to me from Ms. Truth, a fourth-grade teacher in Los Angeles, reveals the magnitude of this undertaking:

> Today was an almost unbearably sad day at school. According to my students (all of which were SOBBING) two young men were sitting in a car yesterday afternoon. Some men in a car rolled up, got out and shot one in the eye (his head exploded) there was a 3-month old in the back seat (she was left "unharmed") the other got out and ran (they call him "baby" Marcus) the guys ran after him and shot him in the back and then more when he fell...The nephew of one is

in my class, the brother of the other is in Mr. [Randall's] class. This is a close community so word spread pretty rapidly yesterday. For an hour and a half [this morning] the kids all just talked and cried. I felt ill-equipped to handle a crisis like this but, we got through it...I said as little as possible, I cried with the kids, we all consoled each other, and others began sharing different stories of violence and loss. In the end, I did what I thought (and hope) was best, tried to empower them with the belief that they must work to become the warriors who combat the senseless violence and madness on the streets...We're making cards, and going to send a little money to the families. The kids all seem to feel a little better. How would you handle this? It looks as if many teachers didn't say or do much. Feeling a bit weary today.

In most urban schools, there is no formal structure to prepare or support teachers to handle such tragic events. The result is that, as Ms. Truth mentions, most teachers avoid or ignore tragedies that take place in the community. But the effective teachers I have studied do not.

Ms. Truth's class collected over $100 for the family. She delivered the money, along with several cards expressing condolences, at the funeral of one of the murdered young men. Here, effective teaching included literally generating material resources, and in my research I have witnessed underpaid teachers providing laptops, housing, food, supplies, car rides, and links to legal and medical services. But, more importantly, an effective teacher is herself a material resource: an indispensable person who can connect schooling to the real, material conditions of urban life.

SOCRATIC HOPE

West (2001) describes "Socratic sensibility" as the understanding of both Socrates' statement that "the unexamined life is not worth living" and Malcolm X's extension that the "examined life is painful."[3] *Socratic hope* requires both teachers and students to painfully examine our lives and actions within an unjust society and to share the sensibility that pain may pave the path to justice. In my research, effective educators teach Socratic hope by treating the righteous indignation in young people as a strength rather than something deserving of punishment; Freire (2004) called this a "pedagogy of indignation." The moments of despair and rage that urban youth feel are not only understandable, they are, as West (2004) proclaims, an "appropriate response to an absurd situation" (p. 295). He goes on to argue that youth

are saying they want to see a sermon, not hear one. They want an example. They want to be able to perceive in palpable concrete form how these channels will allow them to vent their rage constructively and make sure that it will have an impact. (p. 296)

To show the sermon, rather than preach it, is the essence of Socratic hope.

Darnell, an eleventh-grade student of one of the effective teachers I have studied, explained that this type of teacher-student relationship forms as the result of pedagogy that prioritizes the humanization of students above all else:

In [Mr. Lapu's] class we bonded because we all gave each other a chance to humanize ourselves and let us know each other's stories … [and] after that we looked at each other different. After I told my narrative, I humanized myself and then … they stopped looking at me as just a gang-banger and they started looking at me as a smart black man. I don't want you to acknowledge me as a gang-banger, which happened. I want you to acknowledge me as [Darnell]. He helped us humanize each other, and that's how it was. It was beautiful just knowing that my classmate that's sitting right next to me is fighting the same fight that I'm fighting. So, I got his back. That was beautiful, just knowing that we're going through the same shit. From the 'hood to school. When we walk to school, we gotta dodge a bullet like every day. That's your struggle? Well that's my struggle, too. Let's just handle this right here, so we don't gotta go through this four years from now. We felt comfortable that [Mr. Lapu] had our back, and that's just all it is.

Educators who foster this type of solidarity with and among students recognize the distinction between being liked and being loved by their students. As Ms. Truth explained, being liked comes from avoiding unpleasant situations, whereas being loved is often painful:

Many of these teachers are so afraid that students won't like them if they discipline them that they end up letting students do things that they would never permit from their own children. They lower their standards and will take any old excuse from students for why they did not do their homework, or why they cannot sit still in class or do their work. Not me. You gotta work in my class. I can be unrelenting at times, probably even overbearing. Oh, I might give a student slack here or there, but most of the time I'm like, "go tell it to someone else because I'm not trying to hear that from you right now. We've got work to do."

For urban youth, their evaluation of which side of the loved-liked line an educator stands on is often based on whether we share the painful path with them: Do we make the self-sacrifices in our own lives that we are asking them to make? Do we engage in the Socratic process of painful scrutiny about these sacrifices? Do we have the capacity and commitment to support students when they struggle to apply that framework in their lives? Teachers who meet these challenges are beloved by students. The sacrifices they make and the solidarity it produces earn them the right to demand levels of commitment that often defy even the students' own notion of their capabilities. Teachers who fall short can be liked but not loved, and this means they are unable to push the limits of students' abilities; they cannot take them down the painful path.

With teachers I have studied, the move from liked to loved did not happen because of the demands they made of students. It happened because of the level of self-sacrifice, love, and support that accompanied those raised expectations. Sometimes this was simple encouragement, but many times it meant amplifying the material hope they were giving to students. This support took many forms: afterschool and weekend tutoring; countless meals and rides home; phone/text/ email/instant messaging sessions; and endless prodding, cajoling, and all-around positive harassment. These additional investments of time and money clarified for students the idea that with raised expectations came the teacher's willingness to sacrifice in order to help students along the way.

The development of these trusting relationships also resulted in these teachers feeling indignant about student failure. They saw student failure as their own failure and, consequently, engaged in painful self-critique to determine more appropriate future actions. They never excused students from their responsibilities, and they never let themselves slip into despair—rather, the Socratic project contributed to their hope that they would be more successful next time. Socrates said that "all great undertakings are risky, and, as they say, what is worth while is always difficult" (Plato, 2003, p. 220). As educators, we must take great risks and accept great challenges if we are going to be effective in urban schools. We must confront our failures and know that no matter what we do in our classrooms, there will still be forms of social misery that confront our students. This kind of self-reflection will be painful, but it is necessary all the same.

AUDACIOUS HOPE

Our nation expends a good deal of effort trying to avoid what Carl Jung (1970) referred to as "legitimate suffering," or the pain of the human experience. The stockpiling of resources in privileged portions of the population so that they may be "immune" to suffering, while heaping the unnatural causes of socially toxic environments onto others, creates undeserved suffering while simultaneously delegitimizing it. In the face of these conditions, critical hope is audacious in two ways. First, it boldly stands in solidarity with urban communities, sharing the burden of their undeserved suffering as a manifestation of a humanizing hope in our collective capacity for healing. Second, critical hope audaciously defies the dominant ideology of defense, entitlement, and preservation of privileged bodies at the expense of the policing, disposal, and dispossession of marginalized "others." We cannot treat our students as "other people's children" (Delpit, 1995)—their pain is our pain. False hope would have us believe in individualized notions of success and suffering, but audacious hope demands that we reconnect to the collective by struggling alongside one another, sharing in the victories and the pain. This solidarity is the essential ingredient for "radical healing" (Ginwright, 2009), and healing is an often-overlooked factor for improving achievement in urban schools.

This is the inescapable challenge before us as urban educators, and it is often misunderstood. Too many of us try to create classroom spaces that are safe from righteous rage, or, worse, we design plans to weed out children who display it. The question we should be grappling with is not how to manage students with these emotions, but how to help students channel them. The way I take on this challenge is by thinking about my classroom as a micro-ecosystem. Ecologists would tell me that to build a healthy micro-ecosystem, I need to understand the principle of interdependency—in short, that both pain and healing are transferable from person to person inside the classroom. They would also note that the classroom is not a closed micro-ecosystem; I should be aware of external toxins that will be carried into it. I have virtually no control over the array of social toxins to which my students are exposed in the meta-ecosystem of our society, but I can control how I respond to them in my classroom. This gives me, and my students, the audacity to hope.

The pain that our young people carry manifests itself in my classroom in a variety of ways. Sometimes it takes an obvious form like an outpouring of emotion, which might even be directed at me or another student. Usually that pain reveals itself more subtly, in the classic forms of depression (fatigue, sadness, or self-deprecation). In these moments, when a child can no longer contain the pain she feels, my response has the potential to add to it or to begin the healing process. We may think that if we send out the "disobedient" child, we have removed the pain from our system. It simply does not work that way. Rather, when we exclude a child, we introduce another social stressor into the microecosystem. We rationalize the exclusion by telling ourselves that we have pulled a weed from the garden, allowing for a healthier environment for the other children to grow. This ignores the fact that every student in our classroom is part of a delicate balance built on interdependency. K. Wayne Yang, an urban science and math teacher for more than seventeen years, and one of the finest educators I have known in my career, put it this way: "All my students are indigenous to my classroom and therefore there are no weeds in my classroom."[4] From this perspective, the decision to remove a child, rather than to heal her, is not only bad for the child but is also destructive to the social ecosystem of the classroom.

I have been teaching long enough to know the enormity of this challenge, particularly because these moments almost always happen when I am convinced we are doing something of the utmost importance in the classroom. But then I think to myself, how did I get to a place where I am prioritizing lesson plans over healing a child in pain? This choice not only ignores my most basic sensibilities as a teacher, it also disregards years of research documenting the importance of self-esteem, trust, and hope as preconditions for positive educational outcomes. As educators we tend to seriously underestimate the impact our response has on the other students in the class. They are watching us when we interact with their peers. When we become frustrated and punish youth who manifest symptoms of righteous rage or social misery, we give way to legitimate doubts among other students about our capacity to meet their needs if they are ever in pain.

At the end of the day, effective teaching depends most heavily on one thing: deep and caring relationships. Herb Kohl (1995) describes "willed not learning" as the phenomenon by which students try not to learn from teachers who don't authentically care about them. The adage "students don't care what you know until they know that you care" is supported by numerous studies of effective educators (Akom, 2003; Delpit, 1995; Duncan-Andrade, 2007; Ladson-Billings, 1994). To provide the "authentic care" (Valenzuela, 1999) that students require from us as a precondition for learning from us, we must connect our indignation over all forms of oppression with an audacious hope that we can act to change them. Hokey hope would have us believe this change will not cost us anything. This kind of false hope is mendacious; it never acknowledges pain. Audacious hope stares down the painful path; and despite the overwhelming odds against us making it down that path to change, we make the journey again and again. There is no other choice. Acceptance of this fact allows us to find the courage and the commitment to cajole our students to join us on that journey. This makes us better people as it makes us better teachers, and it models for our students that the painful path is the hopeful path.

LICENSE TO HOPE AUDACIOUSLY

Obama has given us license to reinsert hope into the mainstream educational discourse. He has called for a "radical transformation" of urban schools, placing emphasis on the "recruitment and training of transformative principals and more effective teachers" (Obama, 2006, p. 161). This will require serious attention to revamping teacher recruitment, credentialing, and support structures so that schools can attract, reward, and retain educators who come to the profession with demonstrated commitments to critical hope. Can we meet such a challenge? Only with a hard look at what hope really means in the lives of urban youth.

There is a well-documented changing of the guard taking place in teaching (NCTAF, 2003) as upward of one million new teachers, mostly in urban schools, will join the profession within this decade. This brings with it an unprecedented opportunity to swing the pendulum toward educational equity. We can, if we so desire, invest heavily in refocusing our efforts to recruit, train, and develop urban educators who are committed to shifting the tide in urban schools from despair to hope. Research in other fields identifies hope as one of the most promising responses to the conditions of urban inequality (Syme, 2004; Wilson, Minkler, Dasho, Wallerstein, & Martin, 2008), suggesting that hope has major implications for successful teaching (and for raising test scores). Educational research suggests that we can know what makes urban educators effective. We can name the characteristics of effective practice. We can link those characteristics to increases in engagement and achievement. If we fail to significantly invest in the support and development of these characteristics in this new wave of teachers, it will not be for lack of know-how but for the lack of determination to provide hope to all our young people.

The radical transformation that Obama is calling for will not occur unless we treat every classroom as having the potential to be a crack in the metaphorical concrete that creates unnatural causes in the lives of urban youth. For those of us who will be working alongside this next generation of teachers, we must purposefully nurture our students, colleagues, and ourselves through the cracks, knowing we will sustain the trauma of damaged petals along the way. It is essential that we understand these damaged petals as the attributes of indignation, tenacity, and audacity. They are not the social stressors we are trying to overcome, and they must not be misinterpreted as deficits in our students. We must implore our colleagues to recognize that our damaged petals, and those of our students, are not what need to be reformed out of us; they are what need to be celebrated about us. Each time we convey this—the true value of the painful path—we are building critical hope in the person next to us who wonders if they, too, can make it through the crack. Obama's campaign has had this galvanizing effect for some, enrapturing the nation with a level of hope that we have not seen for quite some time, particularly among young people. But for me the success of his campaign has been yet another reminder that I teach teachers and I teach the youth in my community because I hope, audaciously.

NOTES

1 This chapter was originally published as Duncan-Andrade, J. (2009). Note to educators: Hope required when growing roses. *Harvard Educational Review*, Vol. 79, pp. 181–194. Reprinted with permission. All rights reserved. Boston: Harvard University.

2 Unless otherwise noted, quotes from teachers and students are from interviews and conversations that took place during my study of exceptional teachers in Los Angeles between 2002 and 2005 (see Duncan-Andrade, 2007).

3 In his 2001 lecture, West credits Malcolm X with this statement. Socrates made this point in section 38A of Plato's Apology of Socrates.

4 I am indebted to Mr. Yang for our extensive conversations about the development of the ideas presented in this essay.

REFERENCES

Adelman, L. (Executive Producer). (2008). *Unnatural causes: Is inequality making us sick?* [Television Series]. San Francisco, CA: California News Reel.

Akom, A. A. (2003). Re-examining resistance as oppositional behavior: The Nation of Islam and the creation of a black achievement ideology. *Sociology of Education, 76*(4), 305–325.

Barthes, R. (1972). *Mythologies*. London: Fontana.

Delpit, L. (1995). *Other people's children*. New York, NY: New Press.

D'Souza, D. (1995). *The end of racism: Principles for a multiracial society*. New York, NY: Free Press.

Duncan-Andrade, J. (2007). Gangstas, wankstas, and ridas: Defining, developing, and supporting effective teachers in urban schools. *International Journal of Qualitative Studies in Education, 20*(6), 617–638.

Freire, P. (1997). *Pedagogy of hope*. New York, NY: Continuum.

Freire, P. (2004). *Pedagogy of indignation*. Boulder, CO: Paradigm.

Garbarino, J. (1995). *Raising children in a socially toxic environment*. San Francisco, CA: Jossey-Bass.

Ginwright, S. (2009). *Black youth rising: Race, activism, and radical healing in urban America*. New York, NY: Teachers College Press.

Jung, C. G. (1970). Psychology and religion: West and east (G. Adler & R. F. C. Hull, Trans.). In G. Adler & R. F. C. Hull (Series Eds.), *Collected works of C. G. Jung* (Vol. 11, 2nd ed.). Princeton, NJ: Princeton University Press.

King, M. L. K., Jr. (1963, August 28). *I have a dream. March on Washington. Washington, DC.* Retrieved February 5, 2009, from http://www.mlkonline.net/dream.html

Kohl, H. (1995). *"I won't learn from you": And other thoughts on creative maladjustment.* New York, NY: New Press.

Ladson-Billings, G. (1994). *The dreamkeepers: Successful teachers of African American children.* San Francisco, CA: Jossey Bass.

Maslow, A. H. (1943). A theory of human motivation. *Psychological Review, 50*(4), 370–396.

McCain, J. (2008). *McCain's concession speech.* Retrieved January 3, 2009, from http://www.nytimes.com/2008/11/04/us/politics/04text-mccain.html

National Commission on Teaching and America's Future. (2003). *No dream denied: A pledge to America's children.* Washington, DC: Author.

Obama, B. (2006). *The audacity of hope: Thoughts on reclaiming the American dream.* New York, NY: Random House.

Plato. (2003). *The republic* (D. Lee, Trans.). London: Penguin Press.

Shakur, T. (1999). *The rose that grew from concrete.* New York, NY: Pocket Books.

Solórzano, D., & Delgado-Bernal, D. (2001). Examining transformational resistance through a critical race and LatCrit theory framework: Chicana and Chicano students in an urban context. *Urban Education, 36*(3), 308–342.

Syme, S. L. (2004). Social determinants of health: The community as empowered partner. *Preventing Chronic Disease: Public Health Research, Practice, and Policy, 1*(1), 1–4.

Valenzuela, A. (1999). *Subtractive schooling.* Albany, NY: SUNY Press.

West, C. (2001). *Progressive politics in these times.* Mario Savio Annual Lecture Series, Berkeley, CA.

West, C. (2004). The impossible will take a little while. In P. Rogat (Ed.), *The impossible will take a while: A citizen's guide to hope in a time of fear* (pp. 293–297). New York, NY: Basic Books.

West, C. (2008). *Hope on a tightrope.* New York, NY: Smiley Books.

Wilson, N., Minkler, M., Dasho, S., Wallerstein, N., & Martin, A. (2008). Getting to social action: The youth empowerment strategies (YES!) project. *Health Promotion Practice, 9*(4), 395–403.

Wright, J. (1990). The audacity to hope. *Preaching Today.* Retrieved February 5, 2009, from http://www.preachingtoday.com/sermons/sermons/audacityofhope.html

MICHELE LÓPEZ-STAFFORD LEVY

9. MARCELINO'S EULOGY

Marcelino was murdered for being Guatemalan—a hate crime like in Charleston, South Carolina June 2015. Like every human being with dignity and respect, Marcelino deserves the eulogy of presidential proportions. Paulo Freire had a deep faith in people. Faith in a better world and possibility as our title suggests. Obama (2015) says, "They did not receive the things promised; they only saw them and welcomed them from a distance, admitting that they were foreigners and strangers on Earth." This eulogy is now given for two incidents of hate crimes within ninety days of each other in the spring and summer of 2015—a snapshot in time.

Because he's undocumented, Marcelino's funeral takes place in the shadows of south Florida. Read this eulogy now with the lens of Guatemalan immigrants who also had promises unfulfilled.

President Barack Obama's Speech and Eulogy for slain Pastor Clementa Pickney:[1]

Giving all praise and honor to God. (Applause.)

The Bible calls us to hope—to persevere, and have faith in things not seen. "They were still living by faith when they died," Scripture tells us. "They did not receive the things promised; they only saw them and welcomed them from a distance, admitting that they were foreigners and strangers on Earth." We are here today to remember a man of God who lived by faith. A man who believed in things not seen. A man who believed there were better days ahead, off in the distance. A man of service who persevered, knowing full well he would not receive all those things he was promised, because he believed his efforts would deliver a better life for those who followed.

To Jennifer, his beloved wife; to Eliana and Malana, his beautiful, wonderful daughters; to the Mother Emanuel family and the people of Charleston, the people of South Carolina. I cannot claim to have the good fortune to know Reverend Pinckney well. But I did have the pleasure of knowing him and meeting him here in South Carolina, back when we were both a little bit younger. (Laughter.) Back when I didn't have visible grey hair. (Laughter.)

The first thing I noticed was his graciousness, his smile, his reassuring baritone, his deceptive sense of humor – all qualities that helped him wear so effortlessly a heavy burden of expectation.

M. López-Stafford Levy (Ed.), Children from the Other America, 97–105.

Friends of his remarked this week that when Clementa Pinckney entered a room, it was like the future arrived; that even from a young age, folks knew he was special. Anointed. He was the progeny of a long line of the faithful – a family of preachers who spread God's word, a family of protesters who sowed change to expand voting rights and desegregate the South. Clem heard their instruction, and he did not forsake their teaching. He was in the pulpit by thirteen, pastor by eighteen, public servant by twenty-three. He did not exhibit any of the cockiness of youth, nor youth's insecurities; instead, he set an example worthy of his position, wise beyond his years, in his speech, in his conduct, in his love, faith, and purity.

As a senator, he represented a sprawling swath of the low country, a place that has long been one of the most neglected in America. A place still wracked by poverty and inadequate schools; a place where children can still go hungry and the sick can go without treatment. A place that needed somebody like Clem. (Applause.)

His position in the minority party meant the odds of winning more resources for his constituents were often long. His calls for greater equity were too often unheeded, the votes he cast were sometimes lonely. But he never gave up. He stayed true to his convictions. He would not grow discouraged. After a full day at the capitol, he'd climb into his car and head to the church to draw sustenance from his family, from his ministry, from the community that loved and needed him. There he would fortify his faith, and imagine what might be.

Reverend Pinckney embodied a politics that was neither mean, nor small. He conducted himself quietly, and kindly, and diligently. He encouraged progress not by pushing his ideas alone, but by seeking out your ideas, partnering with you to make things happen.

He was full of empathy and fellow feeling, able to walk in somebody else's shoes and see through their eyes. No wonder one of his senate colleagues remembered Senator Pinckney as "the most gentle of the forty-six of us – the best of the forty-six of us."

Clem was often asked why he chose to be a pastor and a public servant. But the person who asked probably didn't know the history of the AME church. (Applause.)

As our brothers and sisters in the AME church know, we don't make those distinctions. "Our calling," Clem once said, "is not just within the walls of the congregation, but…the life and community in which our congregation resides." (Applause.)

He embodied the idea that our Christian faith demands deeds and not just words; that the "sweet hour of prayer" actually lasts the whole week long –

(applause) – that to put our faith in action is more than individual salvation, it's about our collective salvation; that to feed the hungry and clothe the naked and house the homeless is not just a call for isolated charity but the imperative of a just society.

What a good man. Sometimes I think that's the best thing to hope for when you're eulogized – after all the words and recitations and resumes are read, to just say someone was a good man. (Applause.)

You don't have to be of high station to be a good man. Preacher by thirteen. Pastor by eighteen. Public servant by twenty-three. What a life Clementa Pinckney lived. What an example he set. What a model for his faith. And then to lose him at forty-one – slain in his sanctuary with eight wonderful members of his flock, each at different stages in life but bound together by a common commitment to God.

Cynthia Hurd.
Susie Jackson.
Ethel Lance.
DePayne Middleton-Doctor.
Tywanza Sanders.
Daniel L. Simmons.
Sharonda Coleman-Singleton.
Myra Thompson.

Good people.
Decent people.
God-fearing people. (Applause.)
People so full of life and so full of kindness.
People who ran the race, who persevered.
People of great faith.

To the families of the fallen, the nation shares in your grief. Our pain cuts that much deeper because it happened in a church. The church is and always has been the center of African-American life – (applause) – a place to call our own in a too often hostile world, a sanctuary from so many hardships.

Over the course of centuries, black churches served as "hush harbors" where slaves could worship in safety; praise houses where their free descendants could gather and shout hallelujah – (applause) – rest stops for the weary along the Underground Railroad; bunkers for the foot soldiers of the Civil Rights Movement. They have been, and continue to be, community centers where we organize for jobs and justice; places of scholarship and network; places where children are loved and fed and kept out of harm's way, and told that they are beautiful and smart – (applause) – and taught that they matter. (Applause.)

That's what happens in church.

That's what the black church means. Our beating heart. The place where our dignity as a people is inviolate. When there's no better example of this tradition than Mother Emanuel – (applause) – a church built by blacks seeking liberty, burned to the ground because its founder sought to end slavery, only to rise up again, a Phoenix from these ashes. (Applause.)

When there were laws banning all-black church gatherings, services happened here anyway, in defiance of unjust laws. When there was a righteous movement to dismantle Jim Crow, Dr. Martin Luther King, Jr. preached from its pulpit, and marches began from its steps. A sacred place, this church. Not just for blacks, not just for Christians, but for every American who cares about the steady expansion – (applause) – of human rights and human dignity in this country; a foundation stone for liberty and justice for all. That's what the church meant. (Applause.)

We do not know whether the killer of Reverend Pinckney and eight others knew all of this history. But he surely sensed the meaning of his violent act. It was an act that drew on a long history of bombs and arson and shots fired at churches, not random, but as a means of control, a way to terrorize and oppress. (Applause.) An act that he imagined would incite fear and recrimination; violence and suspicion. An act that he presumed would deepen divisions that trace back to our nation's original sin.

Oh, but God works in mysterious ways. (Applause.)

God has different ideas. (Applause.)

He didn't know he was being used by God. (Applause.)

Blinded by hatred, the alleged killer could not see the grace surrounding Reverend Pinckney and that Bible study group – the light of love that shone as they opened the church doors and invited a stranger to join in their prayer circle. The alleged killer could have never anticipated the way the families of the fallen would respond when they saw him in court – in the midst of unspeakable grief, with words of forgiveness. He couldn't imagine that. (Applause.)

The alleged killer could not imagine how the city of Charleston, under the good and wise leadership of Mayor Riley – (applause) – how the state of South Carolina, how the United States of America would respond – not merely with revulsion at his evil act, but with big-hearted generosity and, more importantly, with a thoughtful introspection and self-examination we so rarely see in public life.

Blinded by hatred, he failed to comprehend what Reverend Pinckney so well understood– the power of God's grace. (Applause.)

This whole week, I've been reflecting on this idea of grace. (Applause.)

The graceof the families who lost loved ones.

The grace that Reverend Pinckney would preach about in his sermons.

The grace described in one of my favorite hymnals – the one we all know:

Amazing grace, how sweet the sound that saved a wretch like me. (Applause.)

I once was lost, but now I'm found; was blind but now I see. (Applause.)

According to the Christian tradition, grace is not earned. Grace is not merited. It's not something we deserve. Rather, grace is the free and benevolent favor of God – (applause)– as manifested in the salvation of sinners and the bestowal of blessings. Grace.

As a nation, out of this terrible tragedy, God has visited grace upon us, for he has allowed us to see where we've been blind. (Applause.)

He has given us the chance, where we've been lost, to find our best selves. (Applause.)

We may not have earned it, this grace, with our rancor and complacency, and short-sightedness and fear of each other – but we got it all the same. He gave it to us anyway. He's once more given us grace.

But it is up to us now to make the most of it, to receive it with gratitude, and to prove ourselves worthy of this gift.

For too long, we were blind to the pain that the Confederate flag stirred in too many of our citizens. (Applause.)

It's true, a flag did not cause these murders. But as people from all walks of life, Republicans and Democrats, now acknowledge – including Governor Haley, whose recent eloquence on the subject is worthy of praise – (applause) – as we all have to acknowledge, the flag has always represented more than just ancestral pride. (Applause.)

For many, black and white, that flag was a reminder of systemic oppression and racial subjugation. We see that now. Removing the flag from this state's capitol would not be an act of political correctness; it would not be an insult to the valor of Confederate soldiers. It would simply be an acknowledgment the cause for which they fought – the cause of slavery – was wrong– (applause) – the imposition of Jim Crow after the Civil War, the resistance to civil rights for all people was wrong. (Applause.)

It would be one step in an honest accounting of America's history; a modest but meaningful balm for so many unhealed wounds. It would be an expression of the amazing changes that have transformed this state and this country for the better, because of the work of so many people of goodwill, people of all races striving to form a more perfect union. By taking down that flag, we express God's grace. (Applause.)

But I don't think God wants us to stop there. (Applause.)

For too long, we've been blind to the way past injustices continue to shape the present. Perhaps we see that now. Perhaps this tragedy causes us to ask some tough questions about how we can permit so many of our children to languish in poverty, or attend dilapidated schools, or grow up without prospects for a job or for a career. (Applause.)

Perhaps it causes us to examine what we're doing to cause some of our children to hate. (Applause.)

Perhaps it softens hearts towards those lost young men, tens and tens of thousands

caught up in the criminal justice system – (applause) – and leads us to make sure that that system is not infected with bias; that we embrace changes in how we train and equip our police so that the bonds of trust between law enforcement and the communities they serve make us all safer and more secure. (Applause.)

Maybe we now realize the way racial bias can infect us even when we don't realize it, so that we're guarding against not just racial slurs, but we're also guarding against the subtle impulse to call Johnny back for a job interview but not Jamal. (Applause.)

So we search our hearts when we consider laws to make it harder for some of our fellow citizens to vote. (Applause.)

By recognizing our common humanity by treating every child as important, regardless of the color of their skin or the station into which they were born, and to do what's necessary to make opportunity real for every American – by doing that, we express God's grace. (Applause.)

For too long –

AUDIENCE: For too long!

THE PRESIDENT: For too long, we've been blind to the unique mayhem that gun violence inflicts upon this nation. (Applause.)

Sporadically, our eyes are open: When eight of our brothers and sisters are cut down in a church basement, twelve in a movie theater, twenty-six in an elementary school. But I hope we also see the thirty precious lives cut short by gun violence in this country every single day; the countless more whose lives are forever changed – the survivors crippled, the children traumatized and fearful every day as they walk to school, the husband who will never feel his wife's warm touch, the entire communities whose grief overflows every time they have to watch what happened to them happen in some other place.

The vast majority of Americans – the majority of gun owners – want to do something about this. We see that now. (Applause.)

And I'm convinced that by acknowledging the pain and loss of others, even as we respect the traditions and ways of life that make up this beloved country – by making the moral choice to change, we express God's grace. (Applause.)

We don't earn grace.

We're all sinners.

We don't deserve it. (Applause.)

But God gives it to us anyway. (Applause.)

And we choose how to receive it.

It's our decision how to honor it.

None of us can or should expect a transformation in race relations overnight. Every time something like this happens, somebody says we have to have a conversation about race.

We talk a lot about race. There's no shortcut. And we don't need more talk. (Applause.)

None of us should believe that a handful of gun safety measures will prevent every tragedy. It will not. People of goodwill will continue to debate the merits of various policies, as our democracy requires – this is a big, raucous place, America is. And there are good people on both sides of these debates. Whatever solutions we find will necessarily be incomplete.

But it would be a betrayal of everything Reverend Pinckney stood for, I believe, if we allowed ourselves to slip into a comfortable silence again. (Applause.)

Once the eulogies have been delivered, once the TV cameras move on, to go back to business as usual – that's what we so often do to avoid uncomfortable truths about the prejudice that still infects our society. (Applause.)

To settle for symbolic gestures without following up with the hard work of more lasting change– that's how we lose our way again.

It would be a refutation of the forgiveness expressed by those families if we merely slipped into old habits, whereby those who disagree with us are not merely wrong but bad; where we shout instead of listen; where we barricade ourselves behind preconceived notions or well-practiced cynicism.

Reverend Pinckney once said, "Across the South, we have a deep appreciation of history – we haven't always had a deep appreciation of each other's history." (Applause.)

What is true in the South is true for America. Clem understood that justice grows out of recognition of ourselves in each other. That my liberty depends on you being free, too. (Applause.) That history can't be a sword to justify injustice, or a shield against progress, but must be a manual for how to avoid repeating the mistakes of the past – how to break the cycle. A roadway toward a better world. He knew that the path of grace involves an open mind – but, more importantly, an open heart.

That's what I've felt this week – an open heart. That, more than any particular policy or analysis, is what's called upon right now, I think – what a friend of mine, the writer Marilyn Robinson, calls "that reservoir of goodness, beyond, and of another kind, that we are able to do each other in the ordinary cause of things."

That reservoir of goodness.

If we can find that grace, anything is possible. (Applause.)

If we can tap that grace, everything can change. (Applause.)

Amazing grace. Amazing grace.

(Begins to sing) – Amazing grace – (applause) – how sweet the sound, that saved a wretch like me; I once was lost, but now I'm found; was blind but now I see. (Applause.)

Clementa Pinckney found that grace.

Cynthia Hurd found that grace.

Susie Jackson found that grace.

Ethel Lance found that grace.

DePayne Middleton-Doctor found that grace.

Tywanza Sanders found that grace.

Daniel L. Simmons, Sr. found that grace.

Sharonda Coleman-Singleton found that grace.

Myra Thompson found that grace.

Through the example of their lives, they've now passed it on to us. May we find ourselves worthy of that precious and extraordinary gift, as long as our lives endure. May grace now lead them home. May God continue to shed His grace on the United States of America. (Applause.)

Marcelino found that grace. April, 2015 in Lake Worth, Florida—Palm Beach County.

NOTE

[1] Public address. Obama, B. H. (2015, June 26). Eulogy by the President for Reverend Pickney. Retrieved from https://www.whitehouse.gov/the-press-office/2015/06/26/remarks-president-eulogy-honorable-reverend-clementa-pinckney

Figure 1. The home of the slain Guatemalan teen in Palm Beach County, Florida

MICHELE LÓPEZ-STAFFORD LEVY

10. A CRISIS OF POSSIBILITY

> When social change begins it cannot be reversed,
> You cannot un-educate a person who has learned to read,
> You cannot humiliate the person who feels pride,
> And, you cannot oppress the people who are not afraid anymore.
>
> (César Chavez in Griswold del Castillo, 1999)

In the dystopian movie *Elysium,* Neill Blomkamp (2013) creates graphic apocalyptic images of global chaos and the ravages of poverty taking place on the earth of the future—year 2154. The only humans left on earth seem to be depraved, destitute and mostly people of color while the one percent aristocrats lead by actress Jodi Foster orbit above the planet's atmosphere isolated in their own sterile yet elegant oval shaped space station/community called *Elysium.* In this pristine world with super futuristic, innovative medical chambers designed for quick cures for grave injuries and illness with instantaneous, miraculous treatments further dividing the "haves from the have nots" segregating the planet below plagued with all sorts of social ills, immigration and public health calamities and challenges including climate change and environmental issues like droughts, famines, fires, tsunamis, you name it, we got it!

Subtly, the viewers of this film find themselves observing current issues in brilliant ways: public health, the penal system, immigration, classism, sexism, ableism, global warming on and on, *ad nauseum.* In an interview, writer/director Blomkamp stated *Elysium* is a comment on the contemporary human condition. "Everybody wants to ask me about my predictions for the future". The director said, "No, no, no! This isn't science fiction. This is today. This is now."

So much rings true for us living in the 21st century. We hope you enjoyed this tapestry of stories that tell the tales, *cuentos y consejos* about the Central American children who took a great leap of faith in the spring and summer of 2014—numbers we have not seen since the 1980's.

What you did not find in this anthology about the unaccompanied children is tomes of research about immigrants, nor the alphabet soup of DACA, DAPA, Dream Act participants, English acquisition, transitioning to U.S. schools nor reducing people to numbers and statistics with charts and graphs about immigration patterns from Mesoamerica. Rather we attempted to capture a moment in time—2014. There was a tremendous surge of 69,000 children (American Immigration Council) who

M. López-Stafford Levy (Ed.), Children from the Other America, 107–113.

Figure 1. Thirty year resident Maria (seated right) Guatemala Maya Center, Lake Worth, Florida and early childhood caseworker

reached our borders in the spring and summer of 2014. There are people like Maria (see photo) here in Florida for thirty years and promoting early childhood literacy through the feverish work of Father Frank and the Guatemala Maya Center in Lake Worth, Florida.

Rewind from *Elysium's* 2154 to the present century as we RE-SEGREGATE society and U.S schools and like the movie—the one percent peel themselves away from the working poor and the U.S.'s challenge of a shrinking middle class while the laborer from Latin America and Central America builds affordable housing. Short of mayhem in the streets, *Elysium* rings true for so many undocumented immigrants living in poverty who experience being marginalized on a daily basis, "othered" and excluded. We're sure at times being human in post-modern, post-structuralist twenty-first century can be a surreal experience begging questions like what is reality and whose reality is it— daily ontological breakthroughs within an Orwellian existence (Snowdon) and not to mention the enormous profits of standardized testing and the school-to-prison pipeline now featuring family-detention-centers- to-prison-pipeline. Cha ching!

We must stop demonizing youth and help them discover the well of resilience within as they discover their own personal identities and their identities of being U.S. immigrants. Visualize with us, clear paths to citizenship for the undocumented to be able become citizens through hard work, patriotism like the families of U.S. soldiers with clear laws recognizing international driver's licenses. A driver's license is empowering and will aid folks to be resilient—another recurrent, universal theme in immigrant communities (cover photo).

Benard (1993, 1997) described resiliency as the ability to bounce back successfully, despite exposure to severe risks, and as a "self-righting nature" of human development (p. 1). This personal attribute of coping with adversity often requires children to have the following qualities: adaptability, flexibility, cognitive neo-plasticity, social competence, problem solving, autonomy, and a sense of purpose and future (p. 2). Chavkin and Feyl-Gonzalez (2000) stated, "Resiliency theory proposes that all of the attributes are present to some degree in most people. Whether they are strong enough to help individuals cope with adversity, however, depends on the presence of protective factors during childhood" (p. 2).

Richardson, Neiger, Jenson and Kumpfer (1990) have described resilience as "the process of coping with disruptive, stressful, or challenging life events in a way that provides the individual with additional protective and coping skills than prior to the disruption that results from the event" (p. 34). Higgins (1994) echoed this focus in describing resiliency as the "process of self-righting and growth" (p. 1). Wolin and Wolin (1993) defined resiliency as the "capacity to bounce back, to withstand hardships and to repair yourself" (p. 5). They explained that the term "resilient" has been adopted to replace earlier terms used by researchers, such as invulnerable, invincible and hardy because "resilient" recognizes the pain, struggle and suffering involved in the process (Henderson & Milstein, 2003).

Werner and Smith's (2001) ongoing study is a classic about the children of Kauai. Over a 40-year period, they studied 700 at-risk Hawaiian residents born under adverse circumstances, including chronic poverty; about 200 of the sample were considered at high risk. The sample was composed of poor children whose parents and grandparents had immigrated to Hawaii from Asia and Europe. Approximately two-thirds of the sample had various problems during childhood, while the other one-third showed no problems at all. By the time the study participants reached their mid-thirties, almost all (including many who had experienced problems) had become "constructively motivated and responsible adults" (p. 2). A distinguishing factor shared by each of these resilient children was a long-term, close relationship with a caring, responsible adult. "Only about 30 of the original group of 700 did not efficiently 'bounce back'" (p. 4).

Bernard (1991) held that research in child and human development, effective schools and competent communities revealed that successful development in any human system related directly to the quality of relationships (p. 45). Three key characteristics supported productive development: caring relationships, communication of high expectations and positive beliefs and opportunities for participation (p. 57). Werner and Smith (2001) argued the most important of these protective factors was a caring relationship with someone, regardless of whether that person was a parent, teacher or community mentor (p. 12).

In focusing on students and educators, the following definition, adapted by Rirkin and Hoopman (2003), contained elements of resiliency building that should occur:

Resilience can be defined as the capacity to spring back, rebound, successfully adapt in the face of adversity, and develop social, academic, and vocation competence despite exposure to sever stress or simply to the stress that is coherent in today's world. (p. 107)

Henderson and Milstein (2003) believed that every student today—indeed, every person young and old—needed to develop resiliency (p. 7). Families, schools and communities hold the ability to work together to become a resiliency-fostering environment. School communication with the home is a start.

This anthology is a tribute to immigrants who are in detention centers, or who have died or were killed on their journey to the so-called "land of milk and honey". Henry Giroux (2011) states,

For the last decade, we have lived through an historical period in which the United States surrendered its already tenuous claim to democracy. The frames through which democracy apprehends the lives of other human beings worthy of respect, dignity and human rights were sacrificed to a mode of politics and culture that simply became an expression of war, both at home and abroad (p. 137). He goes on, "Under such conditions, basic social supports were replaced by an increase in the production of prisons, the expansion of the criminal justice system into everyday life, and the further erosion of crucial civil liberties." (p. 137)

We'll further that to say the expansion of for-profit detention centers, the U.S. immigration system and the denial of civil liberties like an international driver's license and guest worker passes strips people of basic dignity. There must be progressive solutions for refugees.

Florida is five centuries old, originally discovered, owned and colonized by the Spanish. Here, they found native people in both Florida and their northern neighbors like Georgia and the Crow Indian and Cherokee.

Throughout American history, there were three (3) Seminole Wars and the current Seminole Chief Billy has purchased the global rights to the Hard Rock Casino for the tribe. Needless to say wealthy tribes have great advantages and even greater challenges like apathy, alcoholism and drug addiction but the work of a professor at New Mexico State University (a Mescalero Apache, Pueblo Peoples and Navajo serving institution) looks at Critical Tribal Theory (Haynes-Writer, 2004) and deconstructs hegemonic practices and white authoritarianism for Native Americans.

Indigenous youth have many possibilities for hope. Perhaps the Guatemala Mayan could meet and collaborate with the south Florida Seminole youth and look beyond the artificial lines drawn on maps by white men. One possibility, as our title offers, is the possibility of hope for Indigenous Youth where there is potential for exchanges of ideas about Native American identity and serving the needs of their respective communities.

In the western U.S., Native American scholars like Michael Yellow Bird (2005) speak to the conditions and colonization manifested within our educational institutions:

The U.S. educational system has been one of the most hostile and oppressive aspects of colonialism. Colonized-based educational systems contributed significantly to the destruction of cultural knowledge, and the imposition of the belief Indigenous Peoples and their knowledge and ideas were—and remain—less than those of mainstream peoples. (p. 16)

Of course Yellow Bird's criticism addresses U.S. educational systems about colonization being pushed through the schooling of Indigenous peoples. In a personal communication (2015), Michael stated he was willing to lead and speak to the indigenous youth in south Florida in hopes of a south Florida Indigenous youth conference.

Kincheloe, Slattery and Steinberg (2000) state, "a critical childhood education welcomes and uses the knowledge and institutions children bring to school" (402). The present situation in schools and the future of possibility within the framework of social justice together with literacy to ensure Mesoamerican children is the hope to become more than busboys in restaurants, agricultural workers, landscapers and hotel maids. Possibility itself must be resilient and insistent to be open because if we shut it down, then creating impossibility and the deficit model wins again.

As the subtitle of our anthology suggests, as in all good, sound critical pedagogy, there is hope for the unaccompanied children from Central America for without hope we perish. The focus of our creative collection is about the crisis of possibility in a democracy. The crisis of possibility in our judicial system and immigration courts based in the U.S. fundamental principles of due process and equal protection. The possibility is to be able to self-right and be resilient.

As our snapshots come to a close during the surge of children from Central American trying to connect with their families, a report stated as we went to press, "Earlier this week, Department of Homeland Security (DHS) officials announced a new immigration detention policy that will enable hundreds of women and children who have crossed the southern border illegally to be released from family detention centers if they can prove they are eligible for asylum, prompting a storm of criticism that the end to long-term detention will only exacerbate the border crisis

In their book *Learning a New Land* (2008), the Orozcos and Todorova eloquently state,

All the hopes that the United States has always represented for political freedom, prosperity, and a future that is better than the past continue to be at the heart of each and every immigrant journey. And this is not a one-way street— our society has become ambivalently addicted to the labors of these hopeful newcomers. But immigrants are not simply disembodied arms summoned to the country for their labor—immigrants are human beings and they come with their families or form families once they arrive. Immigrant-origin youth come with big dreams and their initial boundless energies and optimism offer a great, if untapped, national resources. Sensibly and compassionately embracing this wave of our youngest new arrivals will allow them to constructively unleash their great potential to the benefit of all Americans. (p. 377)

In our conversations and discussions with the folks in Jupiter, Lake Worth and Immokalee, the hope of a better life for their progeny was a resounding, recurrent theme. "I didn't have the chance, but I've made it possible for my family to have it". (Personal communication).

We know what drives academia. Merit raises based on publishing for senior faculty, tenure in higher education, research, service and grants are all what the engine of higher education inherited from European traditions. We'd like to thank the scholars Chomsky and Duncan-Andrade for publishing outside the box! So we ask, "When can scholars contribute to eclectic anthologies like ours"? So when can scholars push the limits of their practice besides the studio arts? We attempted to share stories through Web 2.0 like our recorded, unpublished podcast with Peter Roos, or the transcripts from You Tube like Jonathan Ryan with RAICES. We see that it takes a pueblo to coalesce and mobilize when sudden surges of immigrants arrive at our shores and borders—especially unaccompanied minors.

Giroux (2012) in his interview with Bill Moyers asserts, "Hope to me is a metaphor that speaks to the power of the imagination. I don't believe that anyone should be involved in politics in a progressive way if they can't understand to act otherwise, you have to imagine otherwise. What hope is predicated on is the assumption that life can be different than it is now. But to be different than it is now, rather than romanticizing hope and turning it into something Disney-like it really has to involve the hard work of (a) recognizing the structures of domination we have to face, (b) organizing collectively and somehow to change those, and (c) believing it can be done, that it's worth the struggle. If the struggles are not believed in, if people don't have the faith to engage in these struggles, and that's the issue. I mean, working class neighborhood I talked to you about in the beginning of the program, I mean, it just resonates with such a sense of joy for me, the sense of solidarity, sociality. And I think all the institutions that are being constructed under this market tyranny, this casino capitals is just the opposite. It's like that image of all these people at the bus stop, right. And they're all– they're together, but they're alone. They're alone." (Moyers, 2012)

And the drama taking place on stage? What happened to it? In the distance we can see a dark scene with an eerie fog settling on the verdant floor and the drone of a weepy drum can be heard in the background. The clandestine graves in Guatemala's jungles fester just like the ones in Mexico. Just like the mass graves of forty-six teachers! Mother Earth once again closes her weary eyes, clenches her teeth in disgust and rolls over with a painful groan. Will it ever end? There must be hope. There must be possibility for the unaccompanied children who arrived from Central America in the spring of 2014. The crisis of possibility as our title suggests means hope for the children and their families who don't want to be ruled by their fatalism, lack of faith in the possibility of self-determination or control over their lives. An education of domestication or indoctrination and rote memorization fosters conformity to a given social reality, whereas an education consisting of critical thinking, creativity and real-life problem solving fosters transformation and hope for better possibilities. We can indeed effect change. Marcel (1962) profoundly stated, "I hope in thee for us" (p. 12). We hope for a pedagogy of possibility for the unaccompanied minors and their families.

REFERENCES

Benard, B. (1991). *Fostering resiliency in kids: Protective factors in the family, school and community.* Portland, OR: Western Center for Drug-Free Schools and Communities.

Benard, B. (1993). *Turning the corner from risk to resiliency.* San Francisco, CA: WestEd Regional Educational Laboratory.

Benard, B. (1997). Drawing forth resilience in all our youth. *Reclaiming Children and Youth, 6*(1), 29–32.

Blomkamp, N. (2013). *Elysium.* Los Angeles, CA: Sony.

Carcamo, C. (2015, June 24). U.S. policy change may enable speedy release of detained immigrant families. *Los Angeles Times.* Retrieved from http://www.latimes.com/nation/la-na-immigration-family-detention-20150624-story.html

Giroux, H. (2011). *Zombie politics and culture in the age of casino capitalism.* New York, NY: Peter Lang.

Griswald del Castillo, R., & Garcia, R. (1995). *César Chavez: A triumph of spirit.* Norman, OK: University of Oklahoma.

Haynes-Writer, J. (2008). Unmasking, exposing, and confronting: Critical race theory, tribal critical race theory and multicultural education. *International Journal of Multicultural Education, 10*(2), 1–15.

Henderson, N., & Milstein, M. M. (2003). *Resiliency in schools: Making it happen for students and educators.* Thousand Oaks, CA: Sage.

Kincheloe, J., Slattery, P., & Steinberg, S. (2000). *Contextualizing teaching: Introduction to education and educational foundations.* New York, NY: Longman.

Marcel, G. (1962). *Homo viator: Introduction to a metaphysic of hope.* New York, NY: Harper and Row.

Moyers, B. (2013, November 13). *Henry Giroux on 'Zombie politics'.* New York, NY: Moyers and Company (PBS).

Orozco, C. S., Orozco, M. M., & Todorova, I. (2008). *Learning a new land: Immigrant students in American Society.* Boston, MA: Belknap.

Rirkin, M., & Hoopman, M. (2003). *Moving beyond risk to resiliency.* Minneapolis, MN: Minneapolis Public Schools.

Stafford-Levy, M. (2002). Something racial bout washing beans. In C. Garica-Camarillo & R. Rogdriguez (Eds.), *Cantos al sexto sol.* San Antonio, TX: Wings Press.

Werner, E. E., & Smith, R. S. (2001). *Journey from childhood to midlife: Risk, resiliency, and recovery.* New York, NY: Cornell University Press.

Wolin, B., & Wolin, S. (1993). *The resilient self: How survivors of troubled families rise above adversity.* New York, NY: Villard.

Yellow Bird, M. (2005). Decolonizing tribal enrollment. In W. A. Wilson & M. Yellow Bird (Eds.), *For indigenous eyes only: A decolonization handbook* (pp. 179–188). Santa Fe, NM: School of American Research Press.

Something racial bout washing beans
By Michele López-Stafford Levy

Something racial bout washing beans
My hands go on auto pilot
They take over my chore
Suddenly I watch in amazement as they go to work
Removing stones, rinsing the dirt
What a sight to see! Wow! How did I do that?
Memories...
Racial memories...
I think of all the Apache women on my mother's side
The Cherokee on my father's
Then I know
Racial knowledge.
This is what my people did for sustenance
This is what my Indian *abuelitas* and *visabuelas* fed their families
Through winter, spring, summer and fall
Corn,
That's another one.
Helote with red chili and salt
Cornbread dressing with red enchilada sauce.
The color of red brick of course!
I catch myself humming and umming.
While I eat it,
 I realize my people experienced this for
Generations
I hear the moaning of my ancestors
mmm.mmm.mmm.
Rememmmmmmmmmering...
Urging me to keep the stories alive
It's odd to look at my white face
And know
That my heart is *café con leche*
Weirder still
When I taste the food of this valley
Pronounced memories come alive

I won't forget

My *abuelitas* won't let me
May they rest in peace
(From *Cantos Al Sexto Sol*: An Anthology of Aztlanahuae Writings—a banned
collection)

Printed in the United States
By Bookmasters